Unsung Heroes

GET ON WITH IT BY ALGY CLUFF

'At 76, he reflects in this memoir on a blissful-sounding life at home and abroad - high jinks in the Army, languorous City luncheons primed by pink gins, drilling successfully for oil in the North Sea, mining diamonds in Africa and becoming friendly with such disparate figures as Margaret Thatcher and Zimbabwe's notorious President Robert Mugabe...

Enjoyably gossipy, *Get On With It* also contains valuable insights into business and political life... Appropriately, playwright Sir Tom Stoppard suggests his next book should be called *The Importance Of Being Algy*.'

The Daily Mail

'When he was a small boy at boarding school in the 1940s, Algy Cluff's imagination was captivated by hectic tales of derring-do in the novels of John Buchan. He resolved then to actualise this imaginary world of Clubland heroes. For the past half-century he has been, as this rattling, full-throttled, red-blooded memoir shows, a strenuous, venturesome capitalist in Richard Hannay's mould.'   *TLS*

Unsung Heroes
... and a few villains

Algy Cluff

CLUFF & SONS

First published in Great Britain in 2018 by Cluff & Sons
Copyright © John Cluff 2018

John Cluff has asserted his right under the Copyright, Designs and Patents Act 1988 to be identified as the author of this work.

All rights reserved. No part of this publication may be reproduced, stored in a retrieval system or transmitted, in any form or by any means, without the publisher's prior permission in writing.

This book is sold subject to the condition that it shall not, by way of trade or otherwise, be lent, resold, hired out or otherwise circulated without the publisher's prior consent in any form of binding or cover other than that in which it is published and without a similar condition, including this condition, being imposed on the subsequent purchaser.

Every reasonable effort has been made to trace copyright holders of material reproduced in this book, but if any have been inadvertently overlooked the publishers would be glad to hear from them.

Edited, designed and produced by Tandem Publishing
http://tandempublishing.yolasite.com/

ISBN: 978-1-5272-1928-1

10 9 8 7 6 5 4 3 2 1

A CIP catalogue record for this book is available from the British Library.

Printed and bound in Great Britain by CPI Group (UK) Ltd, Croydon CR0 4YY.

To my uncle Bertie, killed at Gallipoli during the First World War, aged seventeen.

And to Gavin Stamp, 1948–2017.

Both Unsung Heroes.

'Things were easier for the old novelists who saw people all of a piece. Speaking generally, their heroes were good through and through, their villains wholly bad.'
W. Somerset Maugham

'There are new words now that excuse everybody. Give me the good old days of heroes and villains, the people you can bravo or hiss. There was a truth to them that all the slick credulity of today cannot touch.'
Bette Davis

'Today we are fighting Communism. Okay. If I'd been alive fifty years ago, the brand of Conservatism we have today would have been damn near called Communism and we should have been told to go and fight that. History is moving pretty quickly these days and the heroes and villains keep on changing parts.'
Ian Fleming

Contents

Preface ... xi
Foreword by Simon Heffer ... xiii

Part I
Thomas Johnston ... 1
The Fighting Parish Family ... 5
Mickie Brand ... 10
Cecil Harcourt ... 15
R. V. Jones ... 23
Michael Stourton ... 30
John Grandy ... 33
Ronald Grierson ... 38
James Rowntree ... 43
'Docker' Boyle ... 45

Part II
Angus Beckett ... 49
Lord Justice Parker ... 65
African Characters ... 69
Derald Ruttenberg ... 73
Nicholas Freeman ... 78
John King ... 82
Geoffrey Keating ... 85

Part III
Clubland Heroes 89
The Spectator 98
Evelyne and Nicholas Berry 102
Tessa Keswick and Patricia Rawlings 111
John Dixon 116
David Tang 118
Rupert Deen 130

The Remembrance Trust 137

Acknowledgements 139
Index 141

Preface

In this, my second book, I hope to continue a trend of producing one volume a year until I am promoted to the great library in the sky!

I joined the Army in 1959 and the City in 1966 and I have been clocking in every morning at 8 a.m. ever since. During those fifty-two years I have met or heard about a rich array of characters, some of whom I present for your diversion in these pages.

In writing this book I have drawn on my own imperfect memory, and therefore ask the reader's indulgence for any errors of fact.

Algy Cluff
London 2018

Foreword

THERE ARE RATHER too many people who, if they think of Algy Cluff, think of him as being a businessman: one of the few survivors of that age in the 1960s and 1970s when Britain was ruled by socialist governments of both parties, and when it took courage and persistence to be an entrepreneur (or a capitalist, as there should be no shame in calling them). As a result, those who made their way in business attracted a kind of glamour and regard that one would hesitate almost terminally to bestow on their successors today. Algy was, and still is, one such glamorous figure, though it would appal him to be described as such. But he is also much more than a businessman: he is a patron of good causes, whether his beloved War Memorials Trust or, perhaps most significant of all, *The Spectator*, which has seldom flourished so vigorously as it did under his tutelage.

But Algy is also a man whose achievements are not marked by any sense of pride or vanity: and when one reads this book one will begin to understand why. He has always been conscious of, and had the most intense respect for, the courage, determination and sacrifice of others; and he has always been able to see humour in the darkest predicament. He has always been fascinated by his fellow man (and woman), and sought to give them credit for what they have accomplished. That is the theme of what follows, though his essays are not always about individuals, but about institutions and organisations. In an age when the most meretricious people carry off awards in honours lists for no reason better than having toadied to a prime minister or being 'famous', remembering those whose forgotten and in some cases undocumented acts have helped their country or the world is a worthy enterprise indeed: and Algy has, in the essays in this book, done the job superbly, by giving recognition where it due and without exaggeration or flannel.

What flows from these pages are not just good stories about fine people, but a strong sense of what the author has in common with them – a sense of humanity and service. He also laments the passing of types that adorned our lives but, in a very different age, hardly now do so at all. Some of those who feature had their characters formed and tested by the Second World War, and took their experiences (rarely discussed, but intensely felt) into business and into clubland – that other place where Algy is in his element – and set the tenor of post-war society.

The essays can be read as elements of autobiography, and useful ones at that, since the light Algy shines on those he had admired (and on a few he has not) says much, subtly, about him. Those who have read his memoir *Get On With It* will meet, often in greater depth, many who had a walk-on part in that work. Algy's experiences in the Far East, the North Sea and especially in Africa are part of the jigsaw of his reminiscences. And inevitably there are larger-than-life figures, whom he captures with a veracity that will be obvious to any who knew them – such as John King, David Tang or the remarkable Tessa Keswick. There are constant touches of sadness in the book because so many of those about whom he writes are dead, and the world they inhabited appears to have gone with them. Happily, Algy survives, and with luck this late flowering of his literary talent has a way to run yet.

Simon Heffer

Part I

Thomas Johnston

When Alex Salmond was Scotland's First Minister and before, alas, he abdicated in favour of Mrs Sturgeon, I was invited by my friend Peter de Vink – Dutch but Scottish by adoption – to a dinner for Salmond at the New Club in Edinburgh. Salmond was on his best form and, if he did not convert all of his guests to the Nationalist cause, he certainly charmed us. The future of North Sea oil featured in the discussion and in particular, understandably, what proportion of its revenue could properly be claimed by Scotland (this was before the decline in oil prices).

After the dinner, Salmond most civilly asked me to cross the road and have a nightcap at Bute House in Charlotte Square – the official residence of the First Minister. He could not have been a more courteous host and the alcohol flowed whilst we talked of oil matters. Firstly, however, he gave me a tour of the treasures of Bute House mostly – as one would expect – paintings by Scotland's finest. They are principally by eighteenth-century artists, although there is one rather striking exception, being a twentieth-century (about 1950) portrait of a handsome male with a shock of silver hair by the English artist Herbert James Gunn. The title bore the legend 'The Rt. Hon. Thomas Johnston, Secretary of State for Scotland 1941–45'. 'I imagine you have never heard of him,' Alex said.

As a matter of fact but not history, I had heard of him, but only because tramping across various Scottish moors over the years I had noticed that many of the reservoirs had plaques recording that they had been opened by Thomas Johnston, then a Labour MP and Chairman of the Scottish Hydro-Electric Board.

Apparently, he ruled Scotland with a rod of iron during the Second World War and worked harmoniously with Winston Churchill. Alex Salmond said, 'You may not know it, but that man gave what may have been the most important dinner of the Second World War, if not the twentieth century.' He then related a story concerning the effect that the war despatches of the defeatist American Ambassador to the UK, Joe Kennedy, were having on President Roosevelt, whose resolve to support Britain was weakening as a result. However, Roosevelt, having recalled Kennedy, agreed to send his close friend and colleague – Harry Hopkins – to Britain to conduct a three-week investigation into the reality of the state of the island's morale and will to fight. Hopkins was conveyed by battleship from Washington to Greenock and was feted by the Prime Minister and the War Cabinet. However, Hopkins was like a clam and revealed none of his impressions.

The day finally came when Hopkins was due to return to Greenock and the American battleship. Churchill signalled Thomas Johnston that the entire War Cabinet were proposing to see him off and try and discern what he was likely to advise Roosevelt. Churchill instructed Johnston to give him the best dinner he had ever had – quite a challenge in Greenock in 2018, let alone in 1940! The dinner duly proceeded and still the American guest of honour played his cards close to his chest. Finally, at the end of the dinner, Harry Hopkins rose to his feet and related these simple but powerful words from the Book of Ruth (1:16–17): 'For whither thou goest, I will go. Thy people shall be my people and thy God, my God. Where thou diest, will I die.' All was well. Every man in the room burst into tears.

Unsung Heroes

***

I discovered verification of this event in the memoirs of Sir Robert Bruce Lockhart. Accordingly I lent my copy to Alex Salmond. I completely forgot that I had done so and some weeks ago I was searching for it fruitlessly in my library. Later I was called by a friend in Edinburgh, who related a strange tale: a friend of his had bought a copy of the memoir, and saw on the flyleaf my very own bookplate. Salmond had, apparently, auctioned off his library and had included the borrowed copy in the sale. The Lockhart memoirs are now safely back home.

The Fighting Parish Family

Many years ago, I decided to dine at the Beefsteak Club. The club has one long table and seated at it was a rather startling figure wearing a bookmaker tweed, a yellow carnation and scarlet socks. I sat down next to him, at which point he turned to me and shouted, 'If you wish to talk to me you must score a direct hit.' It immediately became apparent that this was because he was stone deaf! We shouted at each other for a rather exhausting hour during which I realised that my neighbour was Major Michael Woodbine Parish. As it happened, I had known one of his brothers, Godfrey – a mining engineer. There was a third brother, Charles, and they must have established some sort of record for, during the Second World War, Michael had won the Military Cross, Godfrey the Distinguished Service Cross and Charles the Distinguished Flying Cross, although he was eventually killed, mourned I understand by a great many friends and admirers, especially female ones!

Their father – Clement Woodbine Parish – obtained a legal degree at Oxford and, from 1911 until 1914, worked in F. E. Smith's chambers in Lincoln's Inn. Michael, having visited Rhodesia in 1935, determined that his future lay in the mining industry and, shortly before the war started, he took the opportunity of acquiring shares in two mining investment companies: El Oro and the Exploration Company. Legend has it that, as he departed for the war and five years in the Middle East, Michael asked his father if he could keep an eye on the two companies and, if any stock were offered, to buy it. His father dutifully carried out these instructions and, after an eventful and gallant war service, he returned to find himself the controlling shareholder of both companies. Under his stewardship £267,000 of capital was increased to £75 million by the 1980s without any recourse to shareholders for additional funds. Michael's son, Robin, has continued this unblemished performance as well as continuing his father's habit of penning intelligent and idiosyncratic annual statements which became collectors' pieces. One of his themes was that if you go to war to honour a pledge (saving and liberating Poland) and you fail to do so, you cannot claim to have won the war. He has written of his wartime experiences (*Aegean Adventures*, 1993) and of his physical and moral courage there is no doubt. He was awarded the Military Cross for his heroism during the ill-fated Cretan withdrawal.

Charles Woodbine Parish was the eldest of the three brothers, being born in 1915. After Eton, he worked in the City, but his heart was in the skies and from 1934 he flew in the RAFVR at Gatwick virtually every weekend and joined the RAF immediately upon the outbreak of war. He had a probably unequalled record of fifty-four bombing raids, including the first attack on Berlin. In September 1940, he was the only survivor when his Wellington bomber crashed into the sea. Despite the trauma of the crash, he managed to swim seven miles to shore and, within a week, he was airborne again, bombing Berlin and Calais. For the next three years, Charles was constantly on operational duty bombing Essen, Düsseldorf and the industrial towns of the Ruhr. On 22nd April 1943, Charles was on an operation to bomb the Baltic port of Stettin, his fifty-fourth sortie. The bomber, a Stirling, was fatally attacked by a Messerschmitt. One crew member bailed out but Charles, only days after his twenty-eighth birthday, remained at his post in a doomed endeavour to crash land. He had already been awarded the Distinguished Flying Cross in March 1943 for his inspirational leadership.

Meanwhile, Godfrey, the mining engineer, joined the Fleet Air Arm and was stationed on the aircraft carrier HMS *Eagle* which was protecting the Malta convoys. On one occasion, with three other pilots, they intercepted seventy German and Italian aircraft. For the loss of one aircraft they destroyed twenty of the enemy. The three surviving pilots, including Godfrey, were all decorated with the Distinguished Service Cross. Shortly afterwards, HMS *Eagle* was sunk off Gibraltar and Godfrey was picked up after swimming for two hours. The next day he wrote to his wife: 'Very fit after a good swim'! Godfrey also served on HMS *Furious* on the Russian convoys and at the North African (Oran) landings and was on HMS *Victorious* with the British Pacific Fleet when the war ended. He then made an epic solo flight from Ceylon back to England. I am proud to relate that he became a good friend and shareholder of mine.

There can scarcely be a family possessed of such courage. Alas, their proud father's heart was broken by the death of his son Charles. He privately printed a moving tribute to him which remains in the possession of Godfrey's daughter, Ursula Hollis, who has treasured it since his life too was cut short in 1973 when he was only fifty-four.

Mickie Brand

After Eton, Mickie, aged nineteen, was commissioned into the Coldstream Guards, the seventh member of his family to be so, of which he was justifiably proud. My favourite photograph of him is as a Lieutenant in the Coldstream wearing his medals, which adorned the drawing room at 10 Upper Phillimore Gardens for so many years.

Mickie fought in Italy and was wounded by shrapnel from some sort of German hand grenade in 1944. Fifty years later, Mickie developed a hand grenade of his own, the 'Brand cough', which he often detonated without warning, emptying restaurants, clubs and cinemas, even causing minor heart failure. The most hardened German soldier would have run for cover had Mickie perfected that cough in 1944.

He was invalided home and legend has it that a beautiful nurse took a fancy to the handsome Guards officer and persuaded the authorities that he was not fit for more active service, overseas that is. He then spent two years reading modern European history at New College and Nicky Gage recalls him making frequent visits to Firle with a series of alluring companions. Sussex was far and away Mickie's favourite part of the world. At what point his love affair with books began is not clear, but in 1951 he joined Hatchards which, in those days, had an antiquarian department. Shortly afterwards, David Beaufort created a rare book vehicle for Mickie at Marlborough Fine Art where the legendary Harry Fischer supervised him.

In 1960, Henry Vyner – a genial but profligate friend and cousin – bought the rare books section from Marlborough Fine Art and Mickie was launched as an independent dealer. Building the business was challenging enough for Mickie, but keeping Henry Vyner from raiding the till every Friday on his way to the Clermont Club proved impossible and Leopold Joseph bought Vyner out in 1965.

Mickie rapidly built up a reputation for academic integrity and scholarship which, allied to his extraordinary eye for the individual tastes of his clients, led to his achieving favoured status, particularly with the main American libraries – the Getty, Morgan, Harvard and Yale. As early as 1962, UCLA featured a profile of Mickie in their library journal. Not only did he know his job, but he must have been the best-connected dealer of his time, hence his work for the Badminton, Warwick and Rutland collections, amongst others. Jonathan Gestetner, who acquired Marlborough from Mickie and Leopold Joseph in 1990, testified to Mickie's connections, recalling that, the first morning he shared a desk at Marlborough with Mickie, Mickie had two telephone calls, both from dukes! Rather acidly Gestetner said: 'I suppose your next call will be from the royal family.' Half an hour later, Princess Margaret was put through.

Mickie meanwhile had married dear Laura Smith in 1953. Whilst a paragon as husband and parent, he was also very much the club man and he was amongst a group of friends who lunched together virtually every day for forty years at White's Club or Wiltons restaurant. Alas, all of them are dead. I think, in particular, of John Wilton, Peter Ward, Henry Vyner, Billy Wallace, Robin Muir and David (Lord) Brooke ('Brookie') – his nephew.

Complementing this male companionship, Mickie and Laura were indefatigable and skilled hosts at Phillimore Gardens. I have vivid memories of that dining room and the cavalcade of personalities of those times who frequented it and I had many happy times with them, whether staying with me on the White Cliffs of Dover (often with their children) or in Scotland and on many visits abroad. Never a cross word, and the value of our excursions hugely enhanced by Mickie's scholarship and humour. He was a first-class shot and no mean tennis player. Many is the time we went to the theatre or the cinema from Chekhov to *Oklahoma!*, although latterly the cough, allied to Laura's good-natured propensity to witter on about Lady Pembroke and the Duchess of Northumberland throughout *Swan Lake*, became a slight strain. I was forced to remind her of the occasion F. E. Smith was at the theatre: behind him were two ladies – one of whom could have been Laura – who chatted persistently. F. E. turned around and said: 'I wonder if you would mind speaking up? They are making so much noise on the stage I cannot quite hear what you are saying.'

I used to buy books from Mickie, although I recall one occasion when he and I bought (from Brookie) a library together. Brookie had inherited a collection of mostly travel books from a relation, Sir George Clerk, who I think had been British Ambassador to Turkey.

Brookie was not interested in these books and invited us to buy them. Curiously, Brookie then lived in Sussex Gardens, directly opposite where Mickie ended his years. Whilst Mickie and I were waiting in the hall of the block of flats, Mickie was able to point to an example of Brookie's famously over-developed interest in other people's business. On the table lay the post for the inhabitants of the block of flats – one envelope was addressed to Sir somebody or other, and was marked 'Strictly Private and Confidential'. The letter had, written across it: 'Sorry – opened in error – Brooke'.

Mickie's death heralded the end of a species – the upper-class scholar.

Cecil Harcourt

The vivid city of Hong Kong has always interested me and owes its post-war existence to the despatch exhibited by a true unsung hero – Admiral Sir Cecil Harcourt. Harcourt served during the Second World War in the Mediterranean, the Normandy landings, and in 1941–42 was Captain of the *Duke of York* battleship which conveyed Churchill to his first meeting with Roosevelt. The latter statesman, notwithstanding his patrician origins, was a man of the Left in America and implacably anti-imperialist elsewhere, so it was his intention that the consequences of the Second World War should, as far as possible, include the liberation of Colonial Territories in the British Empire. In the Far East, this would include Hong Kong which, after the defeat of Japan, he intended should be delivered to Chiang Kai-Shek's nationalist anti-communist forces. Had this plan eventuated, Hong Kong would have been subsumed in communist China when Chairman Mao expelled Chiang Kai-Shek's troops from mainland China in 1949.

Harcourt, in command of a cruiser squadron in Far Eastern waters, had other ideas. He was friendly with another unsung hero – Sir George Gater, a noted First World War hero who, at the time, was the senior civil servant in the Colonial Office. They realised that it was imperative for Harcourt's squadron to steam to Hong Kong ahead of the Americans. Harcourt did just that, liberating Hong Kong, instating himself as Commander-in-Chief and military administrator until civilian rule was re-established, and releasing thousands of British and Canadian prisoners of war. Hong Kong remained British until 1997, not 1949, and many people – Chinese and British – have much cause to be grateful to Harcourt, who is commemorated by Harcourt Road, Hong Kong Central (but I doubt whether many people, Chinese or British, know anything about him at all).

When Roosevelt died the new British Prime Minister – Attlee – in fact prevailed on Harry Truman to accept the continuance of British sovereignty. Harcourt was then involved in another less important but unusual incident. It would perhaps be stretching credulity to describe Sir Paul Chater (1846–1926) as an unsung hero, but he was most certainly a distinguished businessman and philanthropist who contributed much to the commercial and cultural history of Hong Kong. An Armenian by descent, he was the architect of the concept of land reclamation in that overcrowded city, being the founder of the Hong Kong Land Company. He was also a cultured man and collected a large quantity of oil paintings and watercolours by the foremost draughtsmen of their time – William Alexander and George Chinnery in particular. This collection, covering China, Hong Kong and Macau in the period 1655–1860, was catalogued by James Orange and published in 1924 and that catalogue is now itself a rare volume. Sir Paul then conceived the public-spirited notion of leaving the collection to the people of Hong Kong. What followed is shrouded in mystery but has assuredly earned the Chater collection a place in the world's art mysteries.

In advance of the Japanese invasion of Hong Kong, which surrendered on Christmas Day 1941, the then Governor, Sir Mark Young, instructed that the more valuable Chater pictures be hidden in the basement of Government House. These instructions were carried out by an Hungarian art restorer, Eugene von Nagy

Kobza, Young's ADC, and a senior executive from the public works department. Since the three all died during the occupation without advising where they had hidden it, the ultimate fate of the collection remains a mystery. Young disclosed that the pictures had been cut out of their frames and inserted in metal tubes. Of the 400 pictures in the collection, seventy-five prints and lithographs have been discovered or handed in, but since 1950 the collection has been silent. To this day, not a single watercolour or oil painting has reappeared as, thanks to the comprehensive quality of the Chater catalogue, art scholars would be immediately alerted. So where is it? Various theories have been advanced: that, in fact, it was never hidden at all but was burnt as firewood by the starving and freezing population; that it is in the vaults of the Bank of Japan (the happiest outcome); or that it was on the *Asok Maru*, a British-built vessel but owned at the time by the Imperial Japanese navy, then en route to Japan, which was sunk some seventy nautical miles off Okinawa by the American submarine *Seawolf*; that it remains hidden in a cave somewhere in Hong Kong's hills; or, finally, that it remains buried in the grounds of Government House.

Step forward Admiral Harcourt who approved a thorough dig, assisted by mine sweepers, of the gardens of Government House, but with no result. On departing Hong Kong Harcourt resumed his distinguished naval career. Although producing no children, his stepdaughter from his first marriage was the handsome leading ballet dancer Diana Gould, who gave up her career to marry Yehudi Menuhin.

***

I visited Hong Kong on numerous occasions in the 1980s and 90s when I was engaged in the quest for hydrocarbons off the coast of China, although I would have been better employed searching for the Chater Collection, as what hydrocarbons there were had mostly dispersed as a result of the absence of any cap rock to seal the oil in traps or reservoirs. At about this time I had got to know a QC, John Beveridge, who remains a good friend.

Beveridge is an unusual man, and whereas his convictions and opinions are strongly held and accordingly give rise to controversy, he nonetheless has a good heart complemented by an excellent brain. The latter descends from his Australian landowner father W. I. B. Beveridge who was Professor of Animal Pathology at

Cambridge from 1947 to 1975 and was a Fellow of Jesus College, where his son studied law before being called to the Bar in 1963.

John has a flamboyant, almost Edwardian, taste in clothes and is undeniably possessed of moral and physical courage, the latter manifest during his time as Master of the Westmeath Foxhounds. Nonetheless, there is something enigmatic about him being in favour of the Establishment whilst keeping it at arm's length and ably representing – when a QC – some of the more egregious celebrities of the day such as 'Tiny' Rowland, with whom he enjoyed a long and profitable professional relationship. He has always been most generous with advice across a dining-room table and is, incidentally, possessed of a unique constitution which enables him to eat a five-course lunch without impairing any of his faculties.

As it happened, our paths also crossed in Hong Kong where he qualified as one of my unsung heroes for his conduct of an inquiry into the controversial circumstances attaching to the mysterious death, allegedly by suicide, of a European police officer – one Inspector MacLennan.

This was a fascinating 'locked doors' mystery that gripped Hong Kong for months. John MacLennan had apparently been alerted by his

Superintendent that he was to be interviewed by the Hong Kong Police Special Investigation Unit for allegedly consorting with male Chinese prostitutes. When the Special Investigation Unit arrived at his police quarters, they found all the doors and windows to his flat locked. They forced entry to discover the unfortunate Inspector dead on his bed, apparently having shot himself five times with a service revolver.

By the time any proper investigation had begun, the body had been cremated and the failure of the Special Investigation Unit to conduct a ballistic investigation further compounded a sense of public outrage. The public announcement of suicide was widely derided and a crusade was led by local councillor, Elsie Elliott, and a Catholic priest, Father McGovern, to determine whether MacLennan had been murdered to prevent him revealing a list of Europeans in police and government who were known to be homosexual. Eventually, Members of Parliament at Westminster, including Robin Cook, also took up the cause and a commission of inquiry chaired by a local Chinese judge, T. L. Yang, and run by John Beveridge QC, was established by the Governor on advice from Attorney General John Griffiths.

When Beveridge arrived in Hong Kong, having been appointed after the inquiry had been going for three weeks, he was shocked to discover that the inquiry was being held in camera without transcripts of the proceedings, and advised strongly that the concerns of the public could only be allayed by an open process.

This objective he achieved, as the inquiry sat for many months in Hong Kong; various levels of pressure were placed on Beveridge to hasten proceedings. Beveridge took evidence from a cavalcade of characters, many part of the seedier levels of Hong Kong life. Not only did he conduct his enquiries with compassion and common sense – thus avoiding the risk of wrongly damaging the reputation of senior Europeans in the judiciary and the police, but he arrived at the unpopular but only possible conclusion – suicide. This event from 1980 has now become part of Hong Kong's gay folklore and, recently, a play by an ex-colleague of MacLennan, Agnes Allcock, has been staged.

R. V. Jones

MANY YEARS AGO there was a television series called *The Onedin Line*. This was about a shipping line – not, as its name might suggest, renowned for the singularity of its meals – based in Liverpool and the various buccaneering adventures which occurred in the mid-19th century. I watched this programme every Sunday evening before returning to London and my own buccaneering activity. When the BBC terminated the programme, I wrote to protest and was courteously advised that it was anyway a drama directed at the 11–18 age group (I was fifty at the time). I had a similar excursion into the joys of children's television when, by chance, in the early 1980s I watched mesmerised as Professor R. V. (Reg) Jones delivered the Christmas Royal Institution lectures on measurement. I had not previously heard of this engaging Professor and discovered that he was the Professor of Natural Philosophy at the University of Aberdeen where, by reason of my North Sea oil activity, I maintained a house near Huntly. I got in touch with him and we became firm friends.

I had not heard of Reg because he had been in academe since 1946, finding the Socialist government – and its propensity towards egalitarianism in the conduct of military scientific intelligence – unworkable. However, I soon realised that not only was he the son of a Grenadier and blessed with a mischievous sense of humour, he was also the father of two arrestingly beautiful daughters. He became a regular guest at my Huntly house.

It quickly became clear to me that he was an unsung hero himself, and furthermore was the guardian of the identity of numerous other unsung heroes, mostly scientists or airmen. Reg was large in stature, sandy in colouring and blessed with a most benign open countenance. I only wish I could once again welcome him to my house with the prospect of a weekend of reminiscing ahead.

The bare facts of his life are as follows. He was born in 1911 and educated at Alleyn's School in Dulwich and subsequently at Wadham and Balliol Colleges, Oxford. His career really began when he was appointed the Assistant Director of Scientific Intelligence at the Air Ministry in

1941. Legend has it that his work quickly came to the attention of the Prime Minister who sent for Reg to attend a scientific meeting at 10 Downing Street. Reg, being both shy and modest and inclined towards practical jokes, assumed that the summons was precisely that and ignored it.

As Reg relates in *Reflections on Intelligence* (1989), his task during the Second World War was primarily directed to anticipate the applications of science to warfare by the Germans and, in particular, the radio beams which guided their Luftwaffe to bomb our cities and the radar to defend the Reich against the Bomber Command counter-offensive and to protect us from attack by the V1 and V2 weapons later in the war. As he describes, these episodes brought him into contact with the highest levels of command, as well as with the heroic exploits of the men and women of the Resistance movements, the airmen who flew the photographic and reconnaissance aircraft, and the cryptographers at Bletchley Park.

As Reg records, one of the most spectacular of many scientific achievements in the twentieth century was that of Professor Frederick Lindemann FRS, later Churchill's scientific adviser, who had a seat in the Cabinet and was appointed to the peerage as Lord Cherwell.

In 1917, Lindemann heroically developed the principles of recovering an aircraft from a spin and, I quote from Reg: 'In order to do so, Lindemann learned to fly to prove his theory of recovery from what had hitherto frequently been a fatal condition. Lindemann was the first pilot to put an aeroplane into a spin intentionally. To get permission to learn to fly he had had to bluff his way through the eyesight test, with one of his eyes being almost blind: while chatting to the examining doctor he had memorised the side of the test card that was showing.' This must be one of the most cold-blooded acts of heroism ever, made somehow more remarkable by reason of the fact he wore an overcoat and a bowler hat during the epic flight!

Two characters from Reg's Second World War stable merit mention here. The first, Derek Jackson, has rightly been the subject, at my suggestion, of a biography by Simon Courtauld – *As I Was Going to St Ives: A Life of Derek Jackson*. A millionaire, when that noun had meaning, he became a Fellow of the Royal Society and was the husband of no fewer than six wives (including the louche Barbara Skelton). He also found time to ride in the Grand National. As a distinguished academic in the field of spectroscopy he did valuable work under Reg Jones' direction to develop the 'Windows' process. This involved dropping tin foil to confuse the Luftwaffe radar beams and contributed to significant protection of human life. Not content with all this, he also joined the Royal Air Force as an observer and was awarded the DFC and the AFC for gallantry.

Another favourite of Reg was pilot officer Harold Jordan who, with his all-Canadian crew, carried out an electronic reconnaissance flight in a Wellington aircraft on 2–3 December 1943. This was designed to investigate the radar systems carried by German night fighters to detect our bombers. The mission was 'outstandingly' dangerous because it involved planning for the Wellington to fly in front of a German night fighter and certainly be attacked by it – again and again. I quote from Reg's account:

> West of Mainz a night fighter's transmissions were detected by the Special Radio Operator, Harold Jordan, and the information was relayed back to England. The fighter immediately attacked and the gunner fired a thousand rounds of ammunition until his turret was out of action and he was hit in the shoulder. Jordan was hit in the jaw, the arm and the eye. Nonetheless, he continued to listen to the night fighter's radar and warned the captain,

Pilot Officer Paulton, as the fighter approached for each attack. Four of the crew of six were badly wounded; the port engine throttle was shot away, the starboard throttle jammed at full power; an aileron and the air-speed indicators were out of action. Yet the Wellington continued to fly. It struggled back to the Kent coast where the wireless operator, Flight Sergeant Bigoray, was pushed out on a parachute over land because the heroic Paulton thought that he might not survive immersion in the sea and the Wellington was too damaged to risk coming down on land. Bigoray carried with him a report confirming that the radar transmission was on the frequency that we expected, in case the original radio message had not got through and the rest of the crew should perish in an attempt to land in the sea. It was typical of the whole crew, all of whom miraculously survived this epic mission, that just as Bigoray was about to be pushed out, and badly wounded as he was, he was not sure that he had left his transmission key in the down position to broadcast the distress signal, and he struggled back into the aircraft to check.

Jordan, the only English crew member, was awarded the DSO, Paulton the DFC and the rest of the crew the DFM.

Reg wrote an important book on intelligence, *Most Secret War*, during his retirement and it is gratifying that he was appointed a Companion of Honour when his distinguished war service became public knowledge shortly before he died.

Michael Stourton

In 1957, Hugh Foot was the Governor of the troubled island of Cyprus. He was one of five Cornish brothers, three of whom achieved separate distinction – he as a diplomat, Dingle as Solicitor General and Michael as the Leader of the Labour Party. The call by the Greek Cypriots for *enosis* – union with Greece – antagonised the island's Turkish population and was judged an act of rebellion by the colonial power. As a result, large quantities of British troops were sent to the island, as I was myself at a later time (1963) when the sympathies of the British soldier I judged to be undoubtedly with the Turkish minority.

In 1957, a regiment of the Household Cavalry was stationed there and high feelings were further inflamed when a young officer, Fox-Strangways, was shot in the back and killed whilst in civilian clothes in Nicosia. (It was his uncle who famously kicked Aneurin

Bevan down the steps of White's Club where he had, perhaps unwisely, been taken to lunch by Air Marshal Slessor.) The Household Cavalry, or the Blues as they were known, were enraged and excessive pressure was put upon Greek Cypriot terrorists to identify the murderers. As it happened, a battalion of my regiment, the Grenadier Guards, were also stationed on the island. (They were commanded by an unpopular officer named Colonel Pat Britten and the young officers joyfully whitewashed the Brittens' married quarters with the legend 'Filthy Brittens go home!') In the battalion there was one Michael Stourton, an officer possessed of some liberal idealism, who was upset by the treatment allegedly being meted out to the terrorist prisoners.

One evening, it happened that Sir Hugh Foot held a dinner party at Government House at which Stourton was one of the guests. Halfway through the dinner, Stourton rose to his feet and delivered himself of a fatal speech: 'Your Excellency, as we dine here you should be aware that defenceless Cypriot prisoners are being tortured by British troops.' He then gave the shocked Governor the precise address and grid reference of where the alleged atrocities were taking place. The Governor, left-wing, but doubtless somewhat of a snob, had an old

Etonian baronet as his ADC, Nicholas Nuttall, who also happened to be in the Blues. The Governor sent for Nuttall and ordered him to summon his armoured car, advising Major Stourton that his accusation was of such a serious nature that it was imperative that he, the Governor, should personally investigate.

Nuttall meanwhile made two calls – one summoning the armoured car and the other alerting the troops that the Governor was on his way. By the time the Governor arrived, no evidence of any dubious activity was apparent. In fact, everyone was apparently asleep. The truth was that the British soldiers had no knowledge or involvement but that a subaltern, Jamie Eykyn (in the company commanded by Stourton), whilst detailed to guard an interrogation centre, became aware that the 'Special Branch' of the police were systematically subjecting Greek Cypriots to forms of torture which led to the death of at least one of them. Eykyn reported what he had seen and heard (screaming) to Stourton. It is to his great credit, as a human being and as a Grenadier, that he took the action he did knowing how this could have cost him his career. He subsequently became a successful partner in Savills, the estate agents.

John Grandy

I FIRST MET John Grandy in 1965 and recall playing tennis in Singapore with him, Geordie Selkirk and Brian Wyldbore-Smith. He was then tri-service Commander-in-Chief and I was an insignificant Captain in the Guards Parachute Company on leave from the Borneo jungle. When I next met him, he had retired from the Air Force and, having been Governor of Gibraltar, he was now the Governor of Windsor Castle. This was something of a sinecure, providing ample time for his two favourite pastimes – sailing and shooting. He was a respected and active member of the Royal Yacht Squadron, but it was on the shooting field that I next met him.

We were both paid-up members of a syndicate that rented a property in Shropshire, owned by the wife of the historian Sir Philip Magnus-Allcroft. The other syndicate members were David Westmorland, a chain-smoking courtier and, at that time, the Chairman of Sotheby's; David Dickson, a genial and successful stockbroker, who skilfully chaired W. I. Carr & Company at the start of the phenomenal growth in Far Eastern stock markets that occurred largely through the drive of the bombastic David Stapleton (immensely pleased with himself, he was given the soubriquet 'Stacpoole' by Patrick Lindsay which, although meaningless, somehow conveyed the impression of a ruthless exhibitionist); and three members of the egregious Tillotson family. Tillotsons was a prosperous paper manufacturing company based in Bolton, of which the three brothers had inherited control. Marcus, of a sour and dyspeptic disposition, was the eldest and ran the business, whilst John and Alan – both incorrigibly homosexual – regarded work with the same apprehension others may regard disease.

At breakfast before a day's shooting, one younger member was regaling the guns with an intimate account of one of his female conquests when Alan turned sickly pale and said: 'Not at breakfast please!' I suppose being also a bachelor, although very much younger, I was judged by them to be a possible target. I was not prepared, nonetheless, when I was invited by John to a dinner in his flat in Albany and found myself in an all-male context and introduced to my 'date', an elderly gay, Sir David Webster, who ran the Covent Garden Opera House for many years. I escaped as soon as I was able and confined myself to lunching with the Tillotsons in future (I subsequently discovered that my friend and fellow gun, Rupert Deen, incorrigibly heterosexual, had had a similar experience in the Tillotson 'set'). Alas, Alan and John both ran through their inheritance and died comparatively impoverished.

John Grandy was amongst the most admirable of men and I remember him with particular respect and affection. He was of the generation who served their country so nobly in the Second World War and, subsequently, in the Cold War. He was born in 1913 and joined the RAF in 1931. In many respects, his early career was an ideal existence, serving in the formative and pioneering days of the RAF, including as an instructor and adjutant of the London University Air Squadron from 1937–39. He deserves great credit for training so efficiently a reservoir of university pilots, many of whom played a pivotal role in the Battle of Britain.

He served operationally throughout the war, including forming and commanding 249 (Fighter) Squadron during the Battle of Britain. He was later awarded the DSO and mentioned twice in despatches. But as he rose in seniority, ultimately becoming Chief of the Air Staff, he constantly had to implement political instructions, mostly cost-cutting, which severely tested his loyalties. Gifted with handsome features and a most attractive personality, he was also a thoughtful, meditative individual – characteristics that served him and his country well during the post-imperial, decolonisation era. He held a number of challenging posts including commanding the British nuclear test task force on Christmas Island, Commander-in-Chief RAF Germany when the Berlin Wall went up, Commander-in-Chief Bomber Command while it still maintained the UK nuclear deterrent and Commander-in-Chief Far East during the confrontation with Indonesia. All of these appointments and many others he conducted with humour and courtesy, coupled with an element of steel. Firm but fair would be an appropriate description. He was the first airman to be appointed Governor and Commander-in-Chief of Gibraltar, and impressed by arriving with typical lack of pomposity sailing his own yacht, previously well-known around the Solent, the *Astra Volante*. He was a much-loved member of the Royal Yacht Squadron (of which one of his sons became Rear Commodore) and he was, most importantly, a family man.

John Grandy's final appointment was as Constable and Governor of Windsor Castle, a huge honour in his eyes and very much more preferable to a senior position in industry. He has not received the approbation due to him: firstly as an operational leader in the Second World War and, secondly, for his Cold War role in senior command appointments including the execution of remorseless and, in many respects, wrongly conceived post-war defence cuts.

Ronald Grierson

In 1994, the French Ambassador gave a lunch party at the London Embassy in honour of Sir Ronald Grierson. During the lunch Ronnie was invested by the Ambassador with the Légion d'honneur, an award, as was said mysteriously, for 'exceptional conduct'. This had occurred during the Second World War and it was judged to be due to Ronnie's uncharacteristic self-effacement that it had taken so long for the award to be gazetted – nearly fifty years after the war was over. It turned out that Ronnie, of German-Jewish origin, had served in the British Special Forces in France, Germany, North Africa and Italy. He had begun the war, having been briefly interned, as an eighteen-year-old private in the Pioneer Corps, where his ability and determination to fight was quickly identified. He ended the war, aged twenty-five, as a Lieutenant-Colonel in the Black Watch having, in the interim, also served in the SAS, thereby demonstrating his extraordinary courage and ability.

It was a touching ceremony at the Embassy and, to Ronnie's credit, I had had no idea before of the intensity of his military service. As it happened, I sat next to a distinguished, if controversial, Jewish art dealer who regaled me with his very different wartime experience. He had been a sergeant in the Intelligence Corps after the Normandy Landings and, mindful of returning to his professional career after the war, he had kept a close eye on the map as the Allies advanced, being aware that certain chateaux contained impressive works of art. He noticed that one in particular should just have been liberated and he requested permission to take a detachment and a three-ton lorry with the intention of filling the lorry up with Old Master paintings. To his horror, upon his arrival twenty enemy soldiers emerged from the building with their hands over their heads and he had to fill the lorry up with young Germans rather than Old Masters. For this he was awarded a medal for gallantry, the Military Medal.

Back to geniune heroes, after the war Ronnie joined the United Nations – the start of a giddy series of job changes. These included: Chairmanship of the Industrial Reorganisation Corporation (designed to bring

British industry 'kicking and screaming into the twentieth century'); Warburgs; the Deputy Chairmanship of GEC; Senior Partner of a firm of stockbrokers; and, finally, a role as the very effective driver of the South Bank concept and a legendary fundraiser for cancer research (he was Chairman of the European Organisation for Research and Treatment of Cancer). I knew him through most of these excursions – the stockbrokers being our advisers, Panmure Gordon. One day, Ronnie asked me to lunch at GEC, then housed in spartan offices in Stanhope Gate. I met him in his office where he treated me to a homily on the extraordinary culture of the company. This included what he referred to as an 'open door' office policy – no one was permitted to shut their office door. As we walked to the open door of the lunch room, I observed that all the offices were open and empty, barring two in which the secretaries sat slumped against their typewriters and clearly asleep!

At that time, I was seeking support for our application for North Sea oil licences in the 1972 licensing round. Ronnie thought that Arnold Weinstock, with his famous interest in horse racing, would react favourably to a gamble in the British North Sea. We had an amiable meeting, but Weinstock spent the entire time discussing the merits of an oil painting he had commissioned of one of his favourite nags. Nothing resulted, but I always admired Ronnie's enthusiasm for new concepts together with the elegant manner with which he articulated such enthusiasm.

This articulation had another side to it, for he had a formidable temper and I suppose he was what we would now call bipolar, flying as he did into uncontrollable rages. Such was the degree of his temper that he was finally banned from travelling by British Airways. Endearingly, in his short memoir *A Truant Disposition* he displays a photograph of himself raging at two police officers at Heathrow in 1956 after arriving late for a Paris-bound flight.

Ronnie, handsome and elegant, was the most energetic man I have met and it was impossible to keep up with him. I once attended a dinner party hosted by Charlie Allsopp and his lovely wife in one of their innumerable London houses. Ronnie, typically, arrived late just as we were going into the dining room. 'Who's that woman over there?' he asked me and then 'And who's that attractive blonde?' I explained who they were and he then said 'Who's that man?'

'It's you Ronnie, it's a mirror!' I said.

Ronnie married lateish in life and very happily to Heather Firmston-Williams who had previously been married to Lord Bearsted of the Shell Oil dynasty. She died relatively young (having borne Ronnie a son, Jacob) and I recall attending her Memorial Service in St George's, Hanover Square. They had been a cerebral and artistic couple and I was surprised to see, in the pew in front of me, a certain handsome peer sobbing during the admittedly moving service. As we left the church, I found myself next to him: 'I didn't know you knew Heather and Ronnie,' I said.

'Who?' he replied.

'The Griersons,' I repeated.

'Oh no, I don't know them.'

'Well what on earth are you doing here?' I said.

'I am representing Lord Hanson,' he replied. Earning his fee too.

Ronnie's life was a whirlwind – heroic in his dispatch of bad Germans and pompous bureaucrats and in his relentless work for the general good.

James Rowntree

James Rowntree really belongs in the pages of an Anthony Powell novel – a Major Fosdyke figure. Not much was known of him until he managed to secure a commission in the Life Guards, based solely, legend has it, on the regiment assuming that anyone with his name must enjoy boundless wealth. Portly and reasonably genial, Rowntree not only had no money at all but was really no good at anything either (with one fatal exception) and accordingly he was placed in charge of the officers' mess.

I came to know him as a result of our being nominated by somebody in authority to serve on a Court of Inquiry into the theft of 2,000 used boots! The inquiry was chaired by Major James Chichester-Clark (later Prime Minister of Northern Ireland) assisted by Rowntree and myself. We convened in a Nissen hut at the Guards Depot and, despite it only involving a couple of hours' evidence-taking a day, we managed to spin it out for two or three weeks.

The next time I heard of the luckless captain was quite a shock, as it concerned him being court-martialled for forgery and theft. Unbeknownst to his fellow officers, he did have one outstanding, although unlikely, talent – he was a competent artist. One day he suggested to his commanding officer – Colonel Julian Berry (a very grand and popular figure) – that the painting by Sir Alfred Munnings hanging in the officers' mess dining room needed cleaning on account of the forty years of cigar smoke that it had absorbed. The Colonel gave his assent, whereupon the Captain took the painting to his room, copied it and then delivered the original to an art gallery in Jermyn Street.

Rowntree sold the painting to them for a sizeable sum and placed the copy in the officers' mess dining room. No one noticed any difference until, one morning, Colonel Julian was walking down Jermyn Street on his way to lunch at White's Club and did a double-take as he walked past the window of the gallery. He was rooted to the spot. Could Munnings have painted two identical works? Unlikely, his quick brain calculated. He entered the gallery and the poor Captain's world disintegrated. He was arrested, tried, convicted and imprisoned. Later he committed suicide.

'Docker' Boyle

A VERY DIFFERENT captain indeed was Michael Boyle, known as Docker after Sir Bernard and Lady (Norah) Docker, whose lavish spending excited much press disapproval in the 1950s and '60s. However, all they had in common was the benefit of a great deal of money, inherited, in Docker's case. And there was nothing meretricious about his expenditure. Docker was a most attractive character and, although privileged by birth, and unmistakably privileged by appearance (small and portly but immaculate, with an Edwardian moustache), he was loved by all. His life was bounded by the Irish Guards, Boodle's Club, the Royal Yacht Squadron and the Hampshire Police Authority, of which he was an effective and respected Chairman from 1976 to 1988. His entire life was happily lived within these four confines.

I had the pleasure of serving with him in London when we were charged with mounting the Queen's Guard which, in the 1960s, was a daily event and elicited little interest from the public. There were few, if any, tourists. Docker was the Captain of the Guard on a number of occasions when I was the Ensign. We would mount the guard in the forecourt of Buckingham Palace before marching down the Mall to St James's Palace where we were billeted for twenty-four hours, the guardsmen in a barrack room whilst the three officers – the Captain (a Major), the Subaltern (a Captain) and the Ensign (a Lieutenant) – were housed in some luxury.

It was, and is, the custom for the Captain to invite suitable guests to dinner and the mess, then presided over by the kindly Sergeant (Tom Yardley BEM, something of a legend), benefited from a magnificent cellar. Docker was nothing if not a trencherman and we did ourselves proud. Docker discovered a cache of 1890 brandy in the cellar which it did not take us long to dispose of. I can see him vividly now: immaculate in his mess kit, exuding mischief but never at the cost of his dignity.

He achieved some deserved celebrity as an active sailing member of his beloved Royal

Yacht Squadron and, at one point, he owned and raced two twelve-metres. There exists no one like Docker any more – patrician, kind, competent and selfless.

Part II

Angus Beckett

The story of oil and the UK North Sea remains untold and is populated with heroes (mostly civil servants and oil men) and villains (mostly politicians!). Of the unsung heroes, I would place a civil servant – J. Angus Beckett – at the top of the list. It is easy to forget now the contribution that oil from the North Sea made to our national prosperity and the pioneering work involved. Beckett was the man who devised the licensing process which, in the main, still obtains to this day. This is known as 'the discretionary system' – that is to say North Sea licences are granted at the discretion of the Secretary of State and carry with them varying work commitments. This process has been recently streamlined by the newly established Oil and Gas Authority, to reflect the departure of the major oil companies, but remains largely as Beckett designed it.

The loose chronology of the North Sea saga began in Holland with the discovery of the large Groningen gas field, and was followed by the discovery of oil in Norwegian waters, the Ekofisk fields, in the 1970s. The latter discovery was made by the American Phillips Petroleum Company, whose management deserve approbation for the support they provided to their technical staff who were convinced of the presence of hydrocarbons on a large scale, notwithstanding the expensive failure of a dozen dry holes. By this time – 1970 – it was evident that the UK was sitting on a vast potential reservoir of oil. The authority over this was vested in the petroleum division of what was then known as the Ministry of Fuel and Power. At the head of this division sat Angus Beckett.

The Cambridge-educated Beckett had once written an account of an Icelandic expedition sponsored by the university. Entitled *The Double Traverse of Vatnajokull*, it has become a classic of polar exploration and is offered at £500 per copy now.

Beckett's division was short-staffed, but he rapidly devised the licensing arrangements and divided the UK North Sea into sections – or blocks – 45 square kilometres in dimension. The government, realising the potential, elected to offer over 400 blocks in the fourth round of licensing in 1972. This announcement was initially received with some hostility by the press, but with boundless enthusiasm by the American and Canadian so-called independent oil sector. The press was concerned that these licences should have been more properly auctioned off to the highest bidder, rather than awarded by civil servants on the basis of the work programmes offered and the technical competence of the company concerned. As a compromise, it was conceded that fourteen blocks be auctioned off as an experiment. These bids had to be submitted to the petroleum division in sealed envelopes and were opened by Angus Beckett in the Central Office of Information cinema on Millbank in front of the world's press, Paul Getty and me, amongst many others. The result, although garnering one bid of £11 million from Shell, was deemed inconclusive and has not been heard of again. They then proceeded with the scrutiny of the bids for the remaining three hundred and eighty-six blocks. Unknown to us and the North American companies that had flocked to London, Beckett in his genius had realised that there was a place for all these companies to sustain what he judged to be the optimum objective – to get the North Sea explored as rapidly as possible.

The majors were there too, notwithstanding the Chairman of BP – Sir Eric Drake – delivering himself of the fatuity that he would 'drink every drop of the oil discovered in the North Sea'. In the event, BP and others were handed the most prospective licenses and could hardly avoid discovering oil, so helpful was the geology. But it was the independents who were the real heroes. Alas there was no real British independent oil sector other than a handful of companies – Ultramar and Trinidad Canadian being two of them. Whereas the American oil industry is highly entrepreneurial, regularly losing executives determined to set up their own oil companies, no executives at all left BP or Shell to do so, notwithstanding the government's stated anxiety to support British companies.

Amongst the independents whom Beckett had the wisdom to reward with licences were Siebens, Ranger and Hamilton, all of whom made significant discoveries. Hamilton, however, not only discovered the Argyll Field but also brought it on line themselves using a revolutionary floating production facility; Argyll was therefore the first UK North Sea oil field to produce oil, long before those of the major oil companies.

One of the ploys used by the North American

companies to render their applications more acceptable to Beckett and his staff was to persuade well-known British companies to join their consortium as passive investors. Hamilton co-ventured with Associated Newspapers, to the enormous benefit of the latter group. This came about as follows. Esmond, Viscount Rothermere, grandfather of the present Viscount, was Chairman at the time (1970s) and he had married – as his third wife – Mary Murchison, an American lady, who not only bore him a son (he was seventy-five) but, more importantly, introduced him to her brother-in-law: Fred Hamilton. She has been unkindly described by some as a gold-digger, whereas the reality is that, thanks to her, the Rothermere fortunes were revived significantly. Rothermere, to his credit, made one of the more important entrepreneurial decisions in the family's distinguished history by teaming up with the Hamilton brothers. The Argyll Field produced oil for forty years. Fred Hamilton died recently in Denver, aged eighty-seven.

Esmond Rothermere purchased the estate of Daylesford, which in the eighteenth century had been the seat of Warren Hastings. Rothermere conceived a passion for Warren Hastings and, with the help of Spink & Son, set about building up a collection of paintings by

British artists of Oriental and Indian subjects by Stubbs, the Daniells and William Hodges. They looked magnificent in the Daylesford setting, as I was able to observe when Sunny Marlborough gave a massive ball at Blenheim Palace for his fiftieth birthday and his son Jamie's twenty-first, as I recall.

The guests were put up for the night at various houses in the neighbourhood and fortune had it that I was garaged at Daylesford and placed on Rothermere's right at dinner. We had much to talk about, for I too had formed a consortium to search for North Sea oil. At about the time Hamilton discovered the Argyll Field, my consortium (led by another American, Chris Dohm) – Transworld Petroleum – discovered the Buchan Field. We most reluctantly terminated our conversation and set off for the ball where about the only person I knew, other than the Duke, was his niece – Serena – a statuesque blonde beauty whose mother had married an American naval officer, Captain Ed Russell.

I had had a curious experience at Daylesford whilst changing for dinner and was agog to share it with my fellow revellers. In my bathroom there was, surprisingly, a leather-topped desk of some majesty. I endeavoured to open the drawers and behold what secrets it hid. To my surprise, all the drawers were locked bar one, which opened to reveal £5,000 in cash and a revolver. Heaven knows what was in the locked drawers! The cash was in bundles with labels indicating that it was the proceeds of the sale of some land in Wales, I believe. This was a moment worthy of the pen of P. G. Wodehouse. Was this simply the act of a kindly hostess (at that time – Mary) catering for her guests' every requirement, or did etiquette dictate that I went to her and said: 'Oh, by the way, whilst going through the drawers of your desk, I found some cash and a revolver.' I kept my counsel. The house has changed hands a number of times since Rothermere's death and I have not been invited again. If so, I would make a beeline for that bathroom!

Meanwhile, the North Sea continued to provide mammoth discoveries and, to their credit, BP discovered the Forties Field and others under the leadership of M. M. (Monty) Pennell – an attractive and urbane 'old school' oil man – ably sustained by a team which included some notable figures. Basil Butler was the exploration supremo during those heady days and Dr Jack Birks was the technical director. Matt Linning, a dyspeptic Scotsman, who was two distinct individuals – the pre-Prandial Linning and the Post-Prandial – was the brilliant engineer who oversaw the

Forties development. There were many others including an ex-Foreign Office man, John Grundon, an able negotiator. Our consortium comprised Transworld and the special purpose company CCP North Sea Associates, which I had formed in 1972 with a glittering array of largely aristocratic and wealthy shareholders, which included the egregious Lord Lambton, together with Sunny Marlborough and Lord Reay, to all of whom I had been introduced by Tessa Fraser, then married to Reay and now to Henry Keswick. She is the unsung heroine of those days as it was her imagination and belief in my plans that enabled me to raise the money from such unorthodox sources. Others in the consortium included friends from my Army days, Patrick Lichfield and Nicholas Villiers, together with Nicholas Phillips, Anthony Wigram and Demetri Marchessini.

***

All of these, barring Tessa, Villiers, Wigram and me, are now dead, Marchessini dying whilst on holiday with his grandchildren last February in Tenerife. He slipped on some marble steps and never regained consciousness. He was a controversial man possessed of strong, frequently eccentric, opinions which he unwisely broadcast to an unimpressed world. Notwithstanding a maudlin and misanthropic side to his character, he was a good man with a fine and cultured brain, of whom I became very fond. This side of him was exemplified by his conduct arising from a family tragedy. He had four beautiful and intelligent daughters, three of whom are happily married. The fourth, Tati, had the misfortune to be a passenger in a car in Athens that was involved in a crash, as a result of which she became paralysed and was initially thought to be brain dead as well. I recall accompanying a shattered Demetri to the hospital in St John's Wood to which he had had her flown. From then on – at huge personal financial cost – he never wavered from his duties as a parent, nor did he exhibit any self-pity. I admired him for this and persuaded myself that his more dotty views on life had their origin in his own personal tragedy.

***

Demetri, along with his more balanced younger brother Alexander, had led a gilded life. Both handsome, Demetri in particular, they were thought also to be rich, having inherited their father's fortune established in Greek expatriate tradition through ownership of a family shipping combine – Marchessini Lines – which was skilfully sold at the top of the market. However, by the time of his death, much of this fortune had been dissipated or dedicated to the care of Tati. Demetri only married once, to Lucinda Roberts, and she has been an exemplary mother to all her daughters but virtually heroic in her devotion to Tati. She had the good fortune to be sustained over the years by the incomparable Nicholas Peto – a man of boundless optimism, kindness and some shrewdness.

***

The discovery of the Buchan Field in the central North Sea led to some jubilation, which was quickly tempered by the requirement to fund various step-out wells to confirm the dimensions of the reservoir to the satisfaction of the bankers. The Transworld company had been reorganised following the death of its enterprising founder, Chris Dohm (previously with Amoco), flying his own plane in Florida, and had become jointly owned by three enterprising American companies, two of which were run by delightful individuals – Chase Ritts III and Smiley Raborn, both of whom became close friends. CCP too had permitted its 30 per cent shareholder, Charterhall, to cancel its shareholding by way of a scheme of arrangement allowing them to hold their interest directly on the licence rather than through a shareholding in CCP. This proposal met with some opposition but was finally carried.

The Chairman of CCP, in those days, was Peter A. V. Cooper, whom I had met through his nephew Kevin, a contemporary of mine in the Army. Kevin had been in the Irish Guards, where he determined to conduct himself as a caricature of an Irishman, complete with brogues and an Irish setter. Peter was a tall, handsome old Etonian who had been captured whilst serving with the Coldstream Guards in North Africa. He had been interned in Italy and I sensed that his reluctance to talk about it probably hid a lack of pride rather than modesty. He did tell me once that there was a sort of lassitude that overwhelmed many of the prisoners of war, hardly surprising in the light of their experiences of battle and their inadequate diet. I believe that after his release he served as a staff officer in the Normandy landings and was decorated.

Peter had immense charm and, although fairly laid-back and disinclined to seek out activity, he became a stockbroker of consequence and was the joint senior partner of Myers & Co. when I met him. He was much intrigued by my North

Sea plans and readily agreed to chair CCP, and thus Myers & Co. became our stockbrokers. He was a bachelor and led a charmed life largely constructed around Royal St George's Golf Club in Sandwich (where he died in 1979 at the top of his swing), and where he had one of the four famous Coastguard Cottages. Installed in this house was girlfriend no. 1, Pam Henderson, who resembled a sparrow; whereas girlfriend no. 2, Mona Baring, mother of the wicked Lord Lambton's beautiful girlfriend, was a large comely lady whom he installed in his attractive house – Domaine de la Rose – in Opio in the South of France. During the week he led a bachelor life from a flat in Burton Court in Chelsea.

Myers & Co. made a 'book' in CCP shares and I was rather bewildered when I realised that we had taken the company from an idea to a market value the equivalent of £200 million today within a mere two years. We had much fun in the late 1970s raising money, and it all went to my head. I had had no formal business training and, in 1980, I allowed myself to be distracted by buying *The Spectator* magazine. This caper I have documented elsewhere, but I quickly realised I had neither the time nor the money to allow for me to fulfil my duties to my shareholders (and myself) and to *The Spectator*, whilst certainly having no regrets about owning *The Spectator* for five years and chairing it for twenty-five.

Meanwhile, the circumstances in the North Sea were changing. The appointment of Tony Benn, an unreconstructed Marxist, as the Secretary of State was, we thought at the time, a grave error and had a number of consequences, none helpful. The first of these was the unsettling effect he had on the City and the banks. I have remarked, critically, at my surprise that no executive left Shell and BP to found his own oil company. There were complex reasons for this semi-paralysis, connected with that age not being well disposed towards the entrepreneur. As we know, that has changed. However, the City of London quickly saw the point of the North Sea and, disappointed at the absence of local entrepreneurs raising money, took matters into their own hands and supported the new wave of North American entrepreneurs.

Cazenove were well to the fore in this regard, forging a relationship with Jack Pierce – the founder of Ranger Oil, a small independent that rapidly became a very large independent following the discovery of the giant Thistle Field. Their partner, Michael Belmont, deserves celebration as an unsung City hero in this context. We at CCP were fortunate to receive the support of Barings: their partner Charles Williams, now a distinguished politician and author, had the vision to support us.

However, the City was becoming nervous. Tony Benn then came up with the concept of a British National Oil Corporation which set off alarm bells all over the place. There is nothing intrinsically wrong with an overarching authority and, indeed, we have one now: the Oil and Gas Authority. Nevertheless, there was something coercive and maladroit about the establishment of BNOC, which was dogma-driven and run by an abrasive South African, Alastair Morton, who later ironically became an effective Chair of the Channel Tunnel and one of the businessmen most admired by Mrs Thatcher (who abolished the BNOC in 1982).

By now, my strictures about executives in the major oil companies failing to see the opportunity in the North Sea became otiose as a number of first-class individuals – Tony Craven-Walker and Graham Hearne for example – did just that. However, it was becoming a battle for the independents to raise capital and many of them, including CCP, were acquired by larger and more robust organisations. At this point, I formed Cluff Oil and moved on to offshore China where the industry persuaded itself (wrongly) that the next North Sea equivalent obtained. We have developed an obsession with erecting statues to military heroes – maybe a bust of Angus Beckett, a civilian hero, should be displayed at the office of the Oil and Gas Authority?

A man whom I got to know and like, as a result of my North Sea experiences, was Joe Gormley – then the General Secretary of the National Union of Miners. I was reflecting on the composition of a compelling consortium to apply for licences in the fifth and sixth North Sea licensing rounds and it occurred to me that to team up with the National Union of Miners would have the merit of appealing to the political sensitivities of the then socialist government, whilst providing the doomed mining industry with participation in a growing industry. I wrote Joe a letter, out of the blue as it were, and very soon we began a series of congenial lunch meetings at the White Tower restaurant in Percy Street (alas no more but, for a long time, one of the most popular and reliable restaurants in Soho, run by two glamorous Irish sisters). I confess that the success of these lunches was partially due to my constant companion, alcohol, but I became very fond of Joe – wise and friendly but wary of this gangling Tory entrepreneur.

I wish I had taken notes of our conversations

because I recall that, easy-natured as Joe was, he had not a good word for Ted Heath, claiming that Heath's arrogance was the real cause of what became the miners' strike, and that Heath only had himself to blame. I could well believe this: Joe was the salt of the earth, as we used patronisingly to say, whilst Heath was cut from a very different cloth indeed. I had direct experience of his rudeness as a result of more lunches arranged by Geoffrey Tucker, a genial PR man whose loyalty to Heath was never reciprocated. Joe was enthusiastic about our North Sea idea, but it was derailed by his colleagues who were nervous about the risks and the association with capitalism.

Above: Admiral Cecil Harcourt receiving the Japanese surrender.

Professor R.V. Jones

Sir John Grandy, 3rd from the right.

Sir John Grandy in the cockpit of a Hawker Hunter, 1955.

Man with Cigar – Nicholas Freeman.

Captain Rowntree, soldier and forger.

Martin Russell

Back row: ?, Lord Oliver Poole, ?, Gen. Beresford Pierce, Gen. Sir Brian Horrocks, Geoffrey Keating MC, ?, Field Marshal 'Tiger' Templar, Johnnie Henderson, Brig. E.T. Williams.
Front row: General Sir Oliver Leese, Sir Frank Meggary, Monty, ?, Gen. Freddie de Guingand, ?, Sir Brian Robertson.

AC and John King, Hunthill Lodge, photograph by Andrew Parker-Bowles.

New Year's Eve: Unknown, Geoffrey Keating, David Metcalfe, Lord (Harry) Ashcombe, Mrs Drue Heinz and the 11th Duke of Marlborough.

Malcolm Rifkind, Rutt, AC at the Grannochy, shoot lunch.

Smoke gets in your eyes. Marrakesh. Nicholas Berry, AC, Blondel.

1993, Wedding in Hong Kong.

Evelyne and Nicholas Berry, with Alexander and William.

AC, Peter Phillips, Henry Wyndham, David Ker, Henry Strutt, David Tang and Charles Butter.

Below left: *Spectator* sales trip to Glasgow. AC, Suki Phipps, A. N. Wilson and James Knox. Photograph by Gavin Stamp.
Right: Christopher Booker and AC in the garden of *The Spectator* offices. Presentation of a painting by Lavery to the winner of a competition.

Sonia, Lady Melchett and Lord Lambton.

Johnson Chang and David Tang, beside a portrait of AC.

Tessa Keswick with godson Harry Cluff.

Lord Justice Parker

Her Majesty's Stationery Office publishes, from time to time, the results of investigations into various controversial events in the financial world. I recommend the report of the inquiry, instigated by Edward Heath, into the affairs of Lonrho and, in particular, of its controversial Chief Executive 'Tiny' Rowland. His domination of the inspectors, assisted by his amazing capacity for recollection of the most trivial detail, led to the inquiry failing in its real objective – to terminate Rowland's career. In fact, Rowland – disdained by the Establishment but supported by an army of small shareholders – emerged triumphant, seeing off both the inspectors and the so-called 'straight eight' of non-executives led by the unfortunately named Sir Basil Smallpeice – famously dubbed by Rowland as 'lights on a Christmas tree'. Although Rowland was undeniably a controversial figure, there was something heroic about his unrelenting clashes with the world of smugness and complacency.

Another HMSO report that repays reading and, indeed, is something of an historic document, is the inquiry into the Bank rate change in 1957, chaired competently by Lord Justice Parker. This inquiry, despite its absurd origins, revealed for the first time to the public the manner in which the City of London conducted its business and was, in reality, the origin of the keen focus on what is now called 'insider dealing', although all the witnesses here were correctly exonerated by the wise judge. It also highlighted the role of financial journalists for the first time, leading to many of them, previously obscure, becoming household names. Amongst these were: Fred 'under the clock' Ellis of the *Daily Express*; Patrick Sergeant of the *Daily Mail*; and, more recently, Ivan Fallon, Kenneth Fleet and Anthony Hilton.

The day after the change in the Bank rate was announced, by chance a junior and self-important civil servant, John Pumphrey, joined the London train at Woking and got into the same carriage as a Miss Chataway with whom he was acquainted socially. She worked in some minor capacity at Conservative Central Office and was sister to Christopher Chataway, celebrated athlete and subsequently Tory Member of Parliament. Pumphrey and Miss Chataway exchanged pleasantries during which she made reference to the change in the Bank rate. Exactly what she said is unknown, but the zealous Pumphrey jumped to the conclusion that Miss Chataway (and Conservative Central Office) had had advance warning of the change. Without advising Miss Chataway, he went straight to the Shadow President of what was then known as the Board of Trade, Harold Wilson, and thereafter the issue became a matter of national importance.

Judge Parker was appointed to chair the investigation into the circumstances which led to the change in the Bank rate and there began a feast for the public as the City and many of its grander members were cross-examined, revealing to an astonished world how the Establishment actually operated. In the event, it became clear not that there was any question of impropriety on the part of the senior City figures but rather that they had behaved impeccably within a system which placed them – as non-Executive Directors of the Bank of England and as Executive Directors of major banks and trading houses which held substantial sums of treasury stock – in highly conflicting circumstances.

The inquiry was held in Church House, Westminster, and the revelations – sometimes rather roughly obtained – by Sir Reginald

Manningham-Buller QC (known by some as 'Bullying-Manner') delighted the press and infuriated the Left. That one of the Bank's directors was shooting grouse together with Nigel Birch, the Economic Secretary to the Treasury, who was very depressed (about the pressure on sterling) and that virtually all the principal witnesses had been at Eton together and were members of White's and Boodle's clubs, added to the fun but also to the realisation that the system did require review and reform, which rendered the inquiry, in my view, a most important event in the post-war history of the City of London.

African Characters

In Zimbabwe, where my company was operating various gold mines, I remember visiting one at Bindura, north of Harare. The mine had recently begun production and an excellent Dutch engineer, Max Kraan, was the mine manager and was proudly escorting me around the plant. We came to the new village shop. Sitting behind the counter, which proffered toothpaste and matches etc. was a large lady cradling a baby in her arms. 'What's this charming child's name?' I asked mendaciously. 'Predicament' she replied firmly. That, I reflected, was a most intelligent choice and could be appropriately applied to all our activities in Africa at the time.

It is now fashionable for left-wing students to decry the achievements of Cecil Rhodes (whilst, in some cases, happily living off the scholarships that he endowed). I am in a little difficulty here, for it was he who inspired in me an interest in Africa and I can scarcely believe what the man had achieved by the time he died at Muizenberg in 1902, aged forty-eight. These achievements included: the foundation of de Beers and Consolidated Goldfields; the Premiership of the Cape Colony; the origin of the horticultural industry in southern Africa; and the foundation of two countries bearing his name – Northern and Southern Rhodesia. He left all his money to fund the Rhodes Scholarships. He was personally courageous and was never armed when engaged in hazardous endeavours, such as the discussions with King Cetawayo in Bulawayo. And during all this he managed to obtain a degree from Oriel College, Oxford. His downfall resulted, ironically, from the ill-fated Jameson Raid, which was directed at the Boer leaders in Johannesburg whose treatment of the 'natives' was far more ruthless than Rhodes'.

In any event, this man founded the African mining industry which was unquestionably an Anglo-Saxon-dominated industry for many years and spawned some remarkable, and doubtless equally unacceptable, commercial giants. Most of these were centred on the gold and diamond industry in South Africa. There is a curious biological feature here which is that only the Oppenheimer family seemed capable of producing male heirs. The Rhodes, Beits, Wernhers, Robinsons, Barnatos and Joels have all disappeared on the distaff side. Good riddance, no doubt, the current students at Oriel College would argue!

There were other remarkable mining pioneers in the rest of Africa, of whom Sir Alfred Chester Beatty was the most remarkable. He continued to identify and develop the copper belt in central Africa, mostly in what is now Zambia and the Democratic Republic of Congo (an oxymoron if ever there was one!), without once visiting the place (he did have a house in Egypt near the pyramids) – a unique and rather incredible approach. He was born an American citizen and flourished in the Californian mining industry. He settled in London (his house is now the Russian Embassy) from which he presided over Selection Trust, a mighty mining house in those days. He was a man of culture and assembled an important collection of Persian miniatures and manuscripts and of Impressionist paintings between the wars.

Unusually amongst his peers, he fathered a son, known as Chet (whom I knew and considered a boring version of the ancient mariner). Sir Alfred, by now a British citizen and knight, intended to leave his collection to Britain but the Treasury was intransigent and President de

Valera took advantage of this by granting him tax-free status and even promising him a state funeral. This promise was duly fulfilled, and the astonished citizens of Dublin watched as Sir Alfred's coffin was carried through their streets. They must have thought him a power behind the IRA. HM Treasury's obduracy similarly drove the Gulbenkian collection to Lisbon and the Thyssen collection to Madrid.

The Anglo-Saxon characteristic of the mining and oil industry persevered until twenty-five years ago. The larger mining companies were, and still are, mostly British, North American or Australian-based. It is curious that there are only a handful of French, Italian and Spanish companies and what there are mostly lie under state control. This is changing fast, and a new generation of African businessmen of strength and intelligence is now apparent. And, of course, the Indians and the Chinese have elbowed aside many previous Anglo-Saxon companies, although the smaller companies still tend to be American, Canadian, British or Australian.

Derald Ruttenberg

Once, in the mid-1980s, I was the guest of the admirable Andrew Tennant on his Aberdeenshire grouse moor which, unusually, abuts the North Sea. Amongst the guests was a fabled American billionaire with the unusual name of Derald Ruttenberg. We were adjured by Andy to be on our best behaviour as Ruttenberg was contemplating the purchase of an important shooting and agricultural estate in Angus (known as the Gannochy) and Andy was looking forward to a cornucopia of shooting invitations for him and his cronies. I was an abysmal grouse shot and spent the morning missing covey after covey.

By reason of the mysteries of the system by which the guns draw lots as to which butt they occupy, it wasn't until after lunch that I found myself in the butt next to Ruttenberg, or 'Rutt' as he was known. By complete chance, five high birds in succession flew above me – all of which, to the amazement of me and my loader, I shot. Rutt was apparently most impressed and advised me in the evening that he had completed the purchase of the Gannochy estate that day and that he had admired my shooting and hoped I would honour him by accepting an invitation to the inaugural Gannochy shoot. I concealed the truth about my poor performance during the rest of the day and became a fixture on the guest list at the Gannochy for many years! He also created an outstanding pheasant shoot there.

Rutt was a Jewish lawyer from Chicago possessed of exceptional intelligence and judgement, as well as being unusually cultivated. He was the first backer of KKR – Kohlberg Kravis Roberts – and somehow made another fortune out of obtaining control of the Chrysler Company. He was nothing if not a snob and soon the aristocracy were beating a path to his open door. Grandees such as Sunny Marlborough, the Keswicks and John (Earl of) Derby became regular guests. Derby, although a respectable shot, seemed devoid of any conversational capacity and, as such, responded to whatever you said to him with the single word 'What?'

Rutt maintained a lavish establishment with the finest food and wine in the Gannochy lodge, which was idiosyncratically decorated by his artistic and friendly wife Janet. I recall one evening Duncan Davidson – a toff as well as a successful businessman whom I had met at Aldershot when we were both officer cadets in 1959 – elected to play backgammon after the day's shooting. Also staying was a rather sententious Scottish peer, Lord Mansfield. Davidson and I mischievously pretended to play for £1,000 a point, duly scandalising his lordship. Many years earlier, Davidson had sought membership of the Royal Yacht Squadron, only to receive a letter from the Commodore, Lord Cathcart, which read 'Dear Davidson, in order to qualify for membership of Britain's premier yacht club, you will need to expose yourself a lot more in the Solent'!

Rutt, although already frail by the time he purchased Gannochy, excelled as a shot, a bridge player and a golfer and was one of the leading lights at the Deepdale Golf Club in Manhasset on Long Island. To say this was a rich man's club would be an understatement. Billionaires abased themselves at the feet of Rutt and his fellow gauleiter, Cramer. To my amazement, Rutt told me one day that I had been elected to this august body but, alas, my golf had much in common with my grouse shooting and I could not justify the considerable outlay involved.

His purchase of the Gannochy followed on from the highly profitable refinancing of the Weir engineering group, led by the agreeable and intelligent Viscount (Willie) Weir. His other financial foray in the UK was less happy and took the form of participation in a zany attempt to take over British American Tobacco, prior to splitting it up in the asset-stripping fashion favoured by the sponsors Jimmy Goldsmith and Kerry Packer. It was called the Hoylake Group and £5 million was the entry price to this club, although Rutt recalled there was no paperwork at all. They had underestimated Patrick Sheehy, the then Chairman of British American Tobacco. In appearance Sheehy was almost a caricature of capitalism – florid, portly and intimidating (he ended every sentence with an interrogatory grunt) – but he was nonetheless clever, and he ran rings around Hoylake. They had wrongly assumed that he lived an extravagant lifestyle on the back of the shareholders, whereas the reality was that he was modest, unassuming and repelled by flamboyant behaviour. He was also terrifying and combative, although those attributes concealed the kindest of hearts.

Alas, Rutt died despite having an agreement with a New York hospital that he would pay them $1 million for every year he survived! He was an exceptional man. Sadly, the Gannochy was sold off and split into dozens of smaller properties.

Nicholas Freeman

One of my dearest friends was Nicholas Freeman. He inherited from his father, Robert (always known as 'the Colonel' in deference to his service in the Royal Marines during the war), the family business, which was concerned with importing Havana cigars, mostly Montecristo, into the UK from Cuba. The firm, despite a few dramas, flourished and is now run by his clever daughter Jemma – my god-daughter.

Part of Nicholas' responsibility was of course to maintain good relations with the mercurial leaders of Cuba. In 1985 he conceived the notion of inviting a delegation of Cuban government officials, including the Foreign Minister and the Governor of the Reserve Bank, to London with the intention of arranging high-level meetings for them with British institutions. He called me one morning in some distress as he was discovering that not many institutions were expressing any interest in meeting the representatives of a communist country … could I help? I said I would do what I could, and duly hosted a lunch in the Cavendish room at Brooks's Club, to which I invited David Tang, Sir Patrick Sheehy and others, including Nicholas Villiers, then employed by the Royal Bank of Canada (the only Western country that retained full diplomatic contact).

This lunch was transformative for David and also for Nicholas, as both of them had the intelligence to sense the opportunity that Cuba presented. David, Nick Freeman and I formed the Pacific Cigar Company and, in no time, David Tang had negotiated the rights to the sale of all Havana brands in the Far East. This became not only a very successful investment, but also a thoroughly entertaining experience as David became friendly with Cuba's elite – from Castro downwards – whilst smoking much of the cigar crop himself! Villiers began a series of visits to Cuba for the profit of his employers (and for the pleasure of Villiers).

I myself had a rather less successful effort at developing their gold industry. There is in fact little gold in Cuba, but there are a few high-grade deposits. My visit, via Jamaica, got off to an inauspicious start when, in torrential rain, I was met at the airport by the state minerals director in an ancient car which not only had no windows, but the door of which I had to hold shut during the journey to the national hotel. They were intensely suspicious but nonetheless we submitted an application.

Nothing happened for two years, by which time we had forgotten all about Cuba – then we suddenly received a telegram to say that we couldn't have a gold-mining licence!

***

Freeman ran Hunters and Frankau with conspicuous flair and success, ably assisted by David Lewis as Chairman and Hambros Bank as shareholders, bankers and advisers. Not unhelpfully, most of the partners were cigar smokers themselves. Freeman was not only a shrewd financier but an accomplished salesman with his charm and an address book that included not just his social friends but virtually every bartender and head waiter in the West End. There was, however, one Epicurean citadel to which he had unsuccessfully laid siege – the clubs owned and run by Mark Birley, the acknowledged king of good taste.

One day, Freeman was overjoyed to receive a command to lunch with the great man at Mark's Club. Convinced that the breakthrough was imminent and that large orders would shortly follow, he set off for lunch with a carnation in his buttonhole and a spring in his step. Lunch proceeded well, although no mention of business was raised by Birley until, at the end of the meal, he wearily lit a cigar (not a Montecristo) and said vehemently in his patrician style, 'Now what the hell are you doing about my planning application for the conversion of Harry's Bar?!'

There followed a silence accompanied by the exhalation of some of the world's most expensive smoke, during which it dawned on both of them that there had been some mistake, as indeed was the case. It transpired that Birley's secretary had invited the wrong Nicholas Freeman to lunch – the Chairman of Hunters and Frankau rather than Councillor Nicholas Freeman, the Chairman of the Westminster Council Planning Department.

John King

I BELIEVE THAT I first met John King shooting at Blenheim Palace in 1980. By this time, he had become something of a legend due to his reorganisation of British Airways at the behest of Margaret Thatcher. He was a formidable figure in the boardroom and on the hunting field, in particular, but he had a definite twinkle in his eye which he reserved for those of whom he approved. Of humble background, he resembled a costermonger, rather than the member of the House of Lords which he became.

During the war, he had been in a so-called 'reserved occupation', being the brilliant managing director of Pollard Ball Bearings: Dr Johnson's dictum that a man always feels ill of himself for not having been a soldier certainly applied to John King. His ferocious courage on the hunting field provided some compensation and he was, for many years, the Master of the famous Belvoir hunt. At Wartnaby Manor in Leicestershire he lived in some style thanks to his money and his second wife's good taste. She was Isabel Monkton, daughter of the 5th Viscount Galway and every inch the aristocrat. His first wife, Lorna, to whom he was devoted and who died in 1969, had borne him three sons and a daughter but was unable to keep up with her husband's lust for life and celebrity. When he was not working or hunting, he was shooting or fishing or playing backgammon, at all of which activities he excelled. Every evening, when in London, he played backgammon at White's Club, always with Henry Cavendish who spent four years in the Royal Flying Corps in the First World War and the rest of his very long life at White's! After the war, John assumed the Chairmanship of Babcock International, a famous name in those days.

John, along with his childhood Yorkshire friends Gordon White and James Hanson, also enjoyed a New York dimension to commercial life, and those friends worked and made merry there. The base from which they conducted their forays into the female population of uptown Manhattan was the elegant Brook Club, to which they were benefactors. The Brook, superbly managed, is a haven in New York and contains a fine collection of

American and British paintings, as well as the most charming private dining room that I know. A very grand club, it has always had a strong British representation on its list of members and, for many years, has been ruthlessly and adroitly chaired by Mungo Meehan – an incomparable personality.

When John retired from British Airways and his health began to fail, he cut a rather forlorn figure and my wife and I became very attached to him and Isabel. We spent many happy days at Wartnaby where they were particularly kind to our sons. I also asked him to join the board of *The Spectator* magazine along with Patrick Sheehy, Norman Tebbit and Christopher Fildes (the latter at least knew something about publishing, unlike the rest of us!). Alas, John and Isabel are now dead and Wartnaby sold. He was one of the outstanding figures of the second half of the last century.

Geoffrey Keating

Major Geoffrey Keating, armed only with a Rolleiflex camera, emerged from the battle for Tobruk with a Military Cross. That camera was his sole companion when, during the later invasion of Sicily and miles ahead of the advancing Allies, he entered Taormina to be confronted by four hundred Italian soldiers. Geoffrey, with his usual élan, told the commanding Colonel that he had been sent to secure their surrender … and the Italians promptly capitulated. A semi-professional gambler, he must have relished those 400-1 odds!

A staunch Catholic, Geoffrey began his explosive journey as a press photographer with the *Daily Sketch* in 1938. On the outbreak of war he became official photographer (with a motorcycle) to the 51st Highland Division. As the BEF fell back to the Channel coast, it became apparent to Geoffrey that all were doomed to capture. The inaptly named General Victor Fortune, Divisional Commander, held an evening briefing and laid out the position with inspissated gloom. Geoffrey put up his hand and asked if he could speak. Fortune said: 'What is it Keating?' with some distaste. 'You are surrounded, you c**t, and I'm off!' Geoffrey said. He jumped on his motorcycle and roared away. The next day the entire Division surrendered, barring one platoon under the command of another unsung hero – Lieutenant Richard Broad. Those men spent the next eleven months on the run, miraculously evading capture until they crossed to Spain.

Geoffrey surfaced in North Africa. For his extraordinary courage during the fall of Tobruk, Montgomery awarded him an immediate Military Cross. Monty paid close attention to Geoffrey's advice on PR, with spectacular results – turning the rudderless Eighth Army into the most efficient fighting force in the war. Geoffrey followed Montgomery to France from D-Day, and was present at the German surrender on Lüneburg Heath.

One of the outstanding photographers of the Second World War (2,500 of his images are in the Imperial War Museum and his daughter, Rima, is soon to arrange an exhibition of his work), his life had many compartments: mysterious emissary to the Middle East and particularly to Sheikh Al Narayan of Abu Dhabi, and BP's shadowy outrider in Iran, Russia and the UK. Retiring from BP in 1974, Geoffrey operated as a one-man intelligence and introductory unit. If at times a touch over-zealous (he once sent me an invoice for £500 for 'introducing' me to one of my oldest friends!), he was constant in his good companionship. Among many friends were Mark and Annabel Birley (later Goldsmith), Sonia Melchett, Tony Lambton, Hugh Rathcavan and Alan Whicker. I remember attending many of his lunches at the small, round dining table at 3 King's Yard, including one for Sir Maurice Oldfield (then 'M') to meet John Le Carré.

Geoffrey's energy was prodigious, as was his intelligence and wit. The sole drawback was that he was an Olympic drinker. For some years *Private Eye* ran 'The Geoffrey Keating award for the most drunken guest at *The Spectator* annual summer party'. The winner, year after year: Geoffrey Keating. Shortly before he died, Geoffrey left the Clermont Club after a backgammon session with Simon Brewer and told the doorman to hail a taxi to convey him to Annabel's nightclub. Since they occupy the same building, this seemed an otiose request, but a taxi was duly persuaded to drive him around Berkeley Square and back.

Geoffrey married Suzi and had a daughter, Rima: they both remain devoted to his memory.

Part III

Clubland Heroes

THE REMORSELESS ADVANCE of political correctness seems to have reduced the number of characters populating London clubs nowadays. The gaming laws also served to reduce the level of gambling, most of which is now conducted in legitimate casinos. Fashion has affected gambling too. When I first joined the St James's Club, for example, in 1959, there was an entire room dedicated to backgammon in which all the tables were active from six until eight every weekday evening. The St James's Club merged with Brooks's where their backgammon room alas is now a waiting room; backgammon is no longer played. It is a great shame as it's a fast-moving game throwing up quite extraordinary swings of fortune. It is a game of skill, notwithstanding that the moves are governed by the throw of two dice. The St James's spawned many international players who, in some cases – Philip Martyn and Claude

Beer for example – made a good living out of the game.

Lord (Joss) Pender and Michael Stoop were my two heroes when I first joined that club. Both courteous, and Joss Pender always sported a pink carnation and had perfect manners as well as being a first-class player. He was the Chairman of Cable and Wireless – in those days a mighty organisation. It did not take the business school morons long to destroy it in the 1980s. Michael Stoop, son of Adrian Stoop – the famed Dutch rugby player and large shareholder in Shell – was clever, charming, brave and bone-idle like so many in that post-war generation. He passed out of Sandhurst with the Sword of Honour and won a Military Cross in Normandy. After the war, his attention seemed confined to the opposite sex and backgammon and little else. It was he who lent the hapless Lord Lucan the car in which Lucan made his final journey after murdering his nanny instead of his wife (I never had much regard for his level of competence). Lucan drove to Newhaven, abandoned Stoop's car and, I believe, embarked on the ferry from which he – Captain Maxwell-like – propelled himself into Davy Jones' locker.

***

The finest backgammon player was another egregious playboy of great charm and zero energy – Rupert Bellville – something of a legend in the 1950s. He was the scion of a family who contrived to make a fortune from mustard and lived at Papillon Hall in Leicestershire. Rupert, a pilot, fought with Franco in the Spanish Civil War where he had many adventures, often as a result of landing his plane behind the Republican rather than the Nationalist lines. After the Second World War, he had an arrangement with the pursers of the Cunard Line to provide him with the passengers listed in the first-class section of the two *Queens*, *Elizabeth* and *Mary*. Bellville would study the lists to see if they included any idle, and preferably stupid, rich. If so, he would embark at Southampton with his briefcase – a backgammon board – and invariably returned a richer man. He died relatively young, certainly not from overwork.

***

One of my favourite characters and a member of White's and Brooks's was Martin Russell, related to the Dukes of Bedford (he was a cousin of my friend Paul Irby, a man of character who at that time was a partner in the stockbroking firm of Vickers da Costa). Martin was the son of Gilbert Russell, a banker, and Maud Nelke, a beautiful, civilised and rich Hungarian-Jewish lady. She purchased Mottisfont Abbey, restored it (commissioning a room decorated by Rex Whistler) and filled it with leading figures in British artistic life for thirty years. She kept a vivid war diary which has recently been skilfully edited by her granddaughter, Emily Russell – *A Constant Heart*.

Martin, a sickly and asthmatic child, sought to join the Rifle Brigade at the start of the war but somehow managed to join the Hampshire Regiment by mistake. A Brigadier Lumley, whilst paying tribute to his niceness, determined that he was unfit for a commission, judging him to be too 'dreamy' and 'unsmart'. At this point Duff Cooper, a friend of Martin's father, stepped in and offered him a post in the new Ministry of Information where Duff was the reigning minister. In July 1941, Duff was appointed Chancellor of the Duchy of Lancaster and charged with the task of advising the government on Far Eastern policy based in Singapore. No sooner had Duff Cooper, with Martin in tow, arrived in Singapore than the Japanese landed on the Malayan peninsula. In December, Admiral Tom Phillips, Commander of the British Grand Fleet and exponent of the maxim that 'only ships sink ships', engaged the Japanese navy without an aircraft carrier and, as a result, virtually all of his command including the battleships *Prince of Wales* and *Repulse* were sunk by Japanese aircraft. At this point, Duff Cooper was ordered back to the UK and left Singapore as the airport was under attack. This inevitably prompted some criticism of him for deserting the sinking ship. Martin gallantly elected to remain, but was strongly advised to somehow 'join up' as otherwise the Japanese might have him shot as a spy. Martin arrived at a typically chaotic compromise by sewing an Army Sergeant's stripes on the sleeve of his tropical suit. In the event, the courageous Martin managed to obtain passage to Ceylon (as it then was) on virtually the last ship to leave Singapore. That was on 13th February 1942.

A month later, after a hazardous journey compounded by shortage of food, they disembarked in Colombo. Martin seems to have immersed himself immediately in Colombo life, working as a cypher clerk with the Intelligence Corps whilst starting a chess club and adopting a group of Sinhalese artists known as the '43 Group', of whom the most prominent was George Keyt, about whom Martin wrote a book. He was despatched finally to Delhi where he is rumoured to have become a member of the local stock exchange. Back finally in London, he developed a keen interest in mining and banking and even founded his own bank – M. B. P. Russell & Co. – where in 1966 I opened an account. Alas, the bank ceased trading in 1981 as a result of stock exchange losses that occurred without Martin's knowledge. The latter part of Martin's life was clouded by this misfortune as he battled unsuccessfully to recover these unauthorised losses from his colleague, a Birmingham solicitor. Martin was an intellectual, but vague and unworldly and should never have engaged in commerce. That said, he was a true original – brave and inquisitive, if charmingly dotty.

***

'Loopy' Whitbread

One of the more extraordinary ornaments of clubland in the 1950s and '60s was H. 'Loopy' Whitbread. Of fairly repulsive appearance, with pendulous jowls and a large paunch, he appeared to have had two eggs for breakfast – one of which he had eaten and the other he had smeared over his old Etonian tie. He was a member of the Whitbread brewing family but, because of the danger he represented to the lift boys and to an endearing tendency to ask what the employees he chanced upon were paid and then promptly responding 'ridiculous – that should be doubled!', he was quietly removed.

Living alone in Englefield Green, he would take a bus every day to London, going first to the St James's Club where he would enquire whether there were any letters for him, which indeed there were as he had written them himself in Englefield Green the previous day.

His only subject was Eton College, about which he knew everything, and he carried a list of all the Etonians in his pocket. 'Did you go to Eton?' was his sole form of greeting. If the answer was yes, he would consult his Etonian list to verify the answer. If no, you were of no interest and he would immediately move on. In the afternoons he became something of a menace to younger members at the Royal Automobile Club swimming pool and by the mid-1960s poor Loopy was heard of no more.

***

One evening at the St James's Club in 1960 they held a backgammon competition. I had just been elected and the Chairman kindly asked me to sit next to him. Not only that, but he also gallantly bid for me in the auction later in the evening. The auction was conducted by Ludovic Kennedy and the Chairman was W. Lionel Fraser – at that time the senior partner of Helbert Wagg, an important City firm. Fraser was tall and imposing, with a fine head of white hair. He was a model of rectitude and wrote an interesting autobiography with the complacent title *All to the Good*. This was published before his art dealer son, Robert, was arrested along with Mick Jagger for possession of drugs. That event was famously recorded by Richard Hamilton and published as a limited edition silk screen print by Editions Alecto. Fraser and Jagger are depicted handcuffed together whilst shielding their eyes from the paparazzi's cameras. Lionel Fraser had died by this time, followed shortly after his release from prison by Robert, of AIDS.

By a curious chance, I played some part in the production of this edition as the proprietors of Editions Alecto, Joe Studholme and Paul Cornwall-Jones, had been introduced to me by Charles Jerdein, an unusual and enigmatic figure who had at one point trained racehorses with Dorothy Paget, then a legend. By this time he had become an art dealer from premises in Albermarle Street. Dapper, sharp and incorrigibly homosexual, Jerdein was a regular at the St James's Club backgammon tables, where I met him. Editions Alecto was an intelligent concept formed to provide signed limited editions of contemporary artists whose original work was rapidly becoming unaffordable. Amongst these artists were David Hockney, Allen Jones, Victor Vasarely, Eduardo Paolozzi and Richard Hamilton. The editions produced at their workshop in Kelso Place were of high quality. However, as Jerdein explained to me, they had a cash-flow problem, partially because they had no retail outlet and partially, he averred, because they were doing the wrong jobs: Studholme was running the business and Cornwall-Jones the marketing, whereas it should have been the other way around. Studholme was an aristocratic, sensitive and attractive character with Eton and Oxford stencilled all over him, whilst Cornwall-Jones, also highly intelligent, was more austere, almost rough. I bought editions by all of their artists and solved their cash-flow issues. Joe and Paul exchanged roles, the business flourished and, ironically, they did their tasks so successfully that their products are now out of reach of the ordinary pocket. Poor Jerdein, whom I liked, just disappeared, as bachelors often do, leaving behind only a memory, evoked in my case by walking along Albermarle Street. I do have an idea that he lived with a male friend in Suffolk for a period.

The Spectator

When Alexander Chancellor was Editor of *The Spectator* and I was the proprietor (wondering what on earth I had let myself in for!) we, together with the publisher James Knox, spent much time wracking our brains about what we could do to raise the magazine's lowly profile (at that time the circulation was no more than 20,000 copies). I had built up a collection of twentieth-century paintings through Andrew Patrick and Simon Edsor of the Fine Art Society and I conceived the crazy idea of offering an oil painting by Lavery as a prize in a literary competition. Crazy, because that painting – which cost me £3,000 – would probably be worth twenty times that nowadays. The prize attracted much attention and was presented by Christopher Booker at a small ceremony in *The Spectator*'s garden. Our self-satisfaction with this event was punctured by a sour letter we received from no less a figure than Graham Greene, deploring the fact that *The Spectator*, a second-class magazine (as he described it), was now offering prizes by a third-class artist!

The 'Parliamentarian of the Year' luncheon was a much more successful campaign to raise the magazine's profile. The honours for this concept are shared between Charles Moore and James Knox. The first lunch was held at the Savoy Hotel and it was a battle to persuade as many as fifty people to attend. The first winner was the rather self-important George Thomas, Speaker of the House of Commons. Knox convinced Matthew Gloag, a whisky distiller, to sponsor the event and everyone had a small bottle of Highland Park in front of them. The lunch was preceded by a sermon on the merits of drinking whisky by Gloag. The gathering was – and is – a very good-natured affair and is now the only occasion during the parliamentary calendar when Left and Right get together and enjoy themselves. The prizes have evolved into many different categories – the one to avoid being 'Parliamentarian to Watch' which seems to lead to oblivion. This lunch is now a massive affair and, I believe, has long passed its twenty-fifth anniversary. During that long period, the magazine has only had two editors after Boris Johnson – Matthew d'Ancona, whose father was a distinguished civil servant in the Ministry of Fuel and Power, whom I knew, and the present incumbent, Fraser Nelson. Both added lustre to the magazine and numbers to the circulation.

We also made a determined effort to build a readership in Glasgow and Edinburgh when A. N. Wilson was the Literary Editor; the desirable and competent Suki Phipps (now Paravicini) the Sales Manager; James Knox the Publisher; and Gavin Stamp the Architectural Columnist.

Gavin has, alas, recently died. He was a heroic figure in the world of conservation, firing broadsides from his base at the Victorian Society and the Twentieth Century Society. His passions were easily aroused and led to the protection of many buildings thought to be doomed. He feared no one and held in particular contempt architects themselves and planning bureaucrats, repeatedly reminding them that buildings belong to all of us. However, I think his real passion was spent on behalf of the soldiers killed in the calamitous First World War. Throughout his life, he waged a verbal war on their behalf which translated into his finest book, *Memorial to the Missing on the Somme*. I asked him to become a trustee of the War Memorials Trust and I was actually writing to him to ask him to join me in the establishment of a new charity,

The Remembrance Trust, when I received an email from A. N. Wilson advising of his death. This book is heralding The Remembrance Trust and is dedicated to the inspiration of Gavin Stamp. His energy and good nature admirably complemented his stimulating companionship. He was always either about to be in a rage about a worthy cause, in a rage already, or subsiding from a rage. He was as much a hero as those brave soldiers whose deaths he so eloquently deplored.

Evelyne and Nicholas Berry

One of the most impressive women whom I have met was Evelyne Prouvost-Berry. She married, as her second husband, my close friend Nicholas Berry. Sadly both of them died within months of each other: Nicholas of cancer on Christmas Day 2016 and Evelyne as a result of a freak bicycle accident near her house on Belle Isle, off Brittany, in July 2017.

Evelyne was the second of five daughters, two of whom were half-sisters, of Jacques Prouvost, son of Jean Prouvost, a prominent French textile and publishing magnate and at one time proprietor of *Paris Match*, *Paris Soir* and *Marie Claire*. Jacques predeceased his father.

Jean lived in some style in the Rue Saint Honoré in Paris and at a shooting lodge, Saint Jean, near Orleans, where he assiduously harried the local wildlife. After the war, owing to a misunderstanding concerning the

Nazis' use of his printing presses, he himself was harried by the communists and, briefly, had to go into hiding. Evelyne married the Comte Arnold de Contades in 1958 and had two daughters and a son, young Arnaud, now managing the publishing empire. She married, secondly, Nicholas Berry of the distinguished *Telegraph* family, thereby merging two leading European publishing dynasties. They had two sons – William and Alexander.

Nicholas was intensely proud of his antecedents and, in particular of course, the illustrious F. E. Smith, 1st Earl of Birkenhead, although, other than a physical resemblance, they had little in common. It was the family's founding father, William Berry, 1st Viscount Camrose, whom I believe had the most influence on Nicholas and who imbued him with the Puritan ethic that always guided and governed his life. Whilst boundlessly generous to an array of individuals and companies, some of them feckless, Nicholas throughout his life maintained an iron self-discipline without ever being censorious of others. Not for him the chateau-bottled claret, the Savile Row suit or the five-star restaurant. Meretricious behaviour was abhorrent to him, as also was any kind of fuss or extreme of emotion. I would characterise Nicholas as an unsung hero – on two levels in particular. Firstly, as the kindest of men: paying school fees, guaranteeing borrowings, rescuing companies. Secondly, he was one of the outstanding, if uncelebrated by choice, value investors of the last thirty years, sustaining a succession of innovative and inspired forays into contexts as diverse as coal and Cuban debt.

I have no wish to re-open old wounds but there is, I am sure, no doubt that had Nicholas been given the opportunity by his father, Lord (Michael) Hartwell, the *Telegraph* would still today be under Berry family control. However, it was not to be, and, hurt but never embittered, Nicholas embarked on an extraordinary cavalcade of commercial conquest. Space does not allow for mention of all of these – in due course I have no doubt that an appropriate biographer will. However, there are two companies – the Manchester Ship Canal and Mintel – which exemplified his genius, his determination and his financial ingenuity.

Nicholas's interest in the Manchester Ship Canal was stimulated by that company's extensive land holdings and further stimulated, no doubt, by the family connection with Birkenhead in the north west. Nicholas developed the theory that property in that part of England was heavily undervalued compared with the south and a correction was inevitable. That surmise was to prove correct. Nicholas acquired a substantial shareholding and was installed as the company Chairman. This involved frequent visits to the Grosvenor Hotel in Chester where he held court and from where he evolved a simultaneous, and also successful, foray into north-western property through Barlows, a company long associated with his friends the Fildes, of which he also became Chairman. Nicholas, however, was not alone in identifying the value contained in the Manchester Ship Canal land portfolio, and he became locked in prolonged combat with a local company – Peel Holdings – which eventually culminated in Nicholas accepting an offer of £33 per share – they had originally cost him £3. This earned Nicholas respect, as well as garnering him a colossal cornucopia of cash that provided him with the working capital to launch many other adventures. Perhaps the most important of these was Mintel.

Mintel had been a small collection of disparate companies in the 1970s and '80s and the component parts, excluding the reports business, were sold when Nicholas typically stepped in to support an emergency rights issue. John Weeks, now Chief Executive, applauds him for identifying the opportunity, describing Nicholas as a gentleman of the old school. His word was his bond and NatWest Bank accepted that and did not subscribe to the issue and Nicholas became the controlling shareholder. Mintel now has a £100 million turnover, with offices in fourteen cities worldwide and almost 1,000 employees. Nicholas took the title of 'owner', ceding the Chairmanship. He travelled all over the world, adhering to punishing schedules, as he and John built the business. Nicholas's favourite question was: 'What did you learn today?', which kept everyone on their toes.

Latterly, he joined the board of the *Daily Mail* and General Trust as a non-executive director. I know he much valued that renewed acquaintance with a business which he understood, working alongside colleagues whom he admired and liked.

Nicholas the man was always charming and positive and blessed with a multitude of friends but was, nonetheless, not an easy man to get to know. He had an unusual trait of keeping his life in separate compartments, and the occupants of these compartments never varied and never met each other. I dined with him, at Rutland Gate or, latterly, Cowley Street, for over fifty years and my compartment, had it had a label, would have been 'miscellaneous financial', for it contained intermittently: Ivan Fallon,

Christopher and Richard Fildes, Neil Collins and Christopher Honeyman Brown, Chairman of the Governors of Stowe when Nicholas and I served on that body – and nobody else. And there were many other compartments whose occupants not only did I not meet, but in many cases had not heard of. In my mind's eye, I see Nicholas vividly now in the dining room at 18 Cowley Street: cheerful, inquisitive and combative, with a bottle of accurately named 'ordinary claret' in front of him.

For over forty years Nicholas was a very regular and welcome weekend guest at our house on the White Cliffs of Dover, along with another friend, also dead – Paddy Pakenham – to whom Nicholas became much attached. Tennis we played winter and summer, day and night sometimes. One afternoon, I recall sitting with Paddy watching Nicholas play tennis with my wife, and remarking that he never failed to return a tennis shot, that he was always in a good and positive mood, and that he seemed ageless. So, we started a joke which ran for many years, to the effect that he wasn't a human being at all but was actually a Martian, and that mission control was on the White Cliffs into which he had to plug himself from time to time! He loved horses, but latterly bicycles; books (never have I seen him seated without a book in his hands); and tennis and ping pong. I can ruefully attest to his talents at those activities as we used to play for works of art or shares in companies. As a result, I have a lot of shares in useless companies, whilst liberally dispersed through various Berry residences there hangs most of my art collection!

If Nicholas had a gap in his fulfilled life, I believe it was his lack of military service. For he was fascinated by military memoirs, particularly by German generals. And what an excellent general he would have made with his enthusiasm, his energy and brains. He once remarked to me that all one really needs in life is a copy of the *Oxford Dictionary* and a Brigade of Guards tie.

***

Whilst Nicholas was advancing his career in London, Evelyne was equally successful at the helm of *Marie Claire* in Paris. One sister, Marie-Laure, died around 2007. In 2000, another sister, Donatienne, wished to sell her shares in *Marie Claire* to the highest bidder along with L'Oreal's 49 per cent stake. Evelyne was in danger of losing control to an outside bidder, but she was able, with help from Nicholas, to buy out both of the shareholders and sell on a minority stake to Lagardere. During this period, Nicholas remained staunchly British and Evelyne visited the UK frequently for weekends. Gradually, this changed and Nicholas became fonder of life in Paris and Sologne.

Over the last thirty-five years, we regularly holidayed together either in Arcachon or, more frequently, at the Hotel du Palais in Biarritz. Every day we would rent an expensive cabana by the hotel swimming pool. Nicholas and I would arrive immediately after breakfast and read or swim (there was a huge rock in the Atlantic around which he would swim, giving the impression that his next landfall would be New York). At lunchtime, Evelyne would descend carrying a book and a pair of headphones. 'Bonjour,' she would say before firmly affixing the headphones and opening the book which she would read throughout lunch. On one occasion, a large wasp interested itself in our lunch, prompting her to remove the headphones and say: 'Kill it Nicky,' before withdrawing to her Trappist refuge.

We often dined in a rustic restaurant in a village called Arcangues where there lived an old admirer of hers – Guy, Marquis d'Arcangues – in his mansion, now a golf club. Guy, small and oriental in appearance, had earned much respect during the war by offering to be exchanged for his aged father who was incarcerated in a German prisoner of war camp. He was also the French amateur golf champion and a poet of celebrity.

Evelyne was variously described after her death as: 'audacious, inspiring and attractive'; 'tenacious and fearless'; and 'direct and wise'. I would use the adjective 'formidable', with corresponding meaning in French and English. *Marie Claire* is her legacy. She acquired it from her father in 1976 and, at her death, it is one of the three largest feminine titles on earth. Evelyne was, rightly, a substantial figure in France's business community and garnered many awards including, in 1987, being voted the Veuve Clicquot Businesswoman of the Year.

Tessa Keswick and Patricia Rawlings

MANY YEARS AGO, when my friend Demetri Marchessini owned the motor yacht *Deineira*, we would cruise regularly around the Greek islands. On one such cruise, two of the girls were Tessa Reay and Patricia Rawlings. I can see them vividly now – in the saloon – nattering away about politics, whilst Demetri and I would smile patronisingly and joke that neither of them had a clue what they were talking about. The girls have had the last laugh as they are now respectively the Baroness Rawlings and Lady Keswick – both distinguished in politics – whilst Demetri and I were non-starters, admittedly willingly so.

Lady (Tessa) Keswick was born a Fraser, the daughter of the 15th Baron Lovat and his wife Rosamund Delves-Broughton. Simon Lovat was not only an aristocrat but he also looked and behaved like one. Of striking appearance, his wartime heroism as the leader of the Lovat

Scouts invested him with added glamour and lustre, as indeed it should as he was awarded the DSO and the MC together with numerous French and Norwegian decorations for gallantry, particularly concerning the St Nazaire Raid. I came to know him through my membership of a dining club, the Shikar Club, which Lovat – together with the splendid Hamish Wallace – ran as Chairman and Treasurer. A sort of upper class cross-talk act between them evolved at the annual dinner of the club, which obtained legendary status.

Lovat and Wallace were both, as is frequently the case, not only distinguished sportsmen but also knowledgeable naturalists, and they set the tone admirably for the Shikar dinners held every December at the Savoy Hotel. They were dedicated to celebrating high standards of conduct where the shooting of large game was concerned. Apart from the fact that the dinners are now held at the Cavalry Club and are chaired by Charles Cecil, ably supported by Chisholm Wallace (Hamish's son), nothing has changed. I have the privilege of having served on the committee for over twenty years. Lovat was always friendly whilst intimidating, but never condescending. I admired both him and Hamish.

Tessa was Simon Lovat's younger daughter

of six children. After a rigorous Catholic education, she married in 1964 the Lord Reay. Reay was a man of good nature and high intelligence but, during the late 1960s, he had become the patient of a Dutch psychiatrist who greatly influenced him for a number of years. This was unfortunate as he had much ability that only surfaced later in life when he became an effective working member of the House of Lords. However, during this period he became introverted and strangely, and disconcertingly, silent. Tessa, who had evolved into a great beauty complemented by intelligence and charm, bore him three children – Aeneas, the current Lord Reay, Ned and a daughter, Laura. She tired of Hugh Reay's behaviour and, never short of admirers, including the writer, began to conduct an independent existence.

Her most persistent suitor, fellow Scottish Roman Catholic patrician and plutocrat Henry Keswick, she finally married in 1985. Before and during her marriage, Tessa developed a keen political sense, contested a parliamentary seat, was elected to a London council and worked as a special adviser to Kenneth Clarke from 1989 to 1995. It was then that she was appointed to direct the Centre for Policy Studies, a centre-right think-tank originally founded by Sir Keith Joseph. She brought considerable flair to this challenge, adding people of intellectual consequence to its advisory board and commissioning numerous pamphlets. As I write, she is the Vice Chancellor of the University of Buckingham and a lady of consequence.

***

Patricia Rawlings is the only child of a successful textile merchant – Louis Rawlings – and his Dutch wife. Louis owned a magnificent flat in Eaton Square, but alas died many years ago. However, his wife, aged 104, and Patricia are still living there. They gave frequent parties in the 1970s, to many of which I was asked. Patricia was the most generous of hostesses. I regret I was rather nervous in those days and drank too much and, as a result, cannot remember as much as I should! However, I met many people who became firm and enduring friends thanks to her unselfish nature.

Patricia got off to an uncertain start with a short-lived marriage to David Wolfson. She is a beautiful woman and happily her youth was captured by Annigoni on a canvas that hangs in Eaton Square. Single and childless, she engaged in good works, particularly for the Red Cross and subsequently for King's College London, of which she became an effective and popular Chairman. This all led eventually to a seat in the House of Lords.

John Dixon

As an only child, I experienced a rather solitary childhood whilst on holidays. My greatest friend for a few years was a 75-year-old widower baronet, Sir John Dixon. After he left Eton, nothing appears to have happened to Sir John at all except attendance at the annual dinner of the Tarporley Hunt Club and occasional spurts of activity at race meetings, of which Chester was preeminent.

He had lived in a large house, Astle Hall, but after his wife's death he moved into a cottage about ten minutes' walk from our house. He had retained the shooting rights to the Astle estate and it was thanks to him that I learnt the elements of shooting. He didn't appear to have any friends, although he was a benign figure, always dressed in Edwardian-style loud check jackets and an old Etonian tie topped off by a tweed cap. He was tall, stooped and boasted a military silver moustache, although he had no military experience, being too young for the First World War and too old for the Second. We used to go rough shooting around the perimeters of his estate. It was fairly marshy ground and occasionally I shot a woodcock, to Sir John's delight. One day, we were advancing two abreast across a sort of bog when there was a yelp and Sir John disappeared from sight, barring his cap. I gingerly placed his stick under one arm and my unloaded gun under the other and, somehow, he managed to lever himself up and out. Had I not been with him, he would certainly have expired, although his crimson countenance suggested he was on the verge of doing so anyway.

When I left Stowe in 1958, I lost touch with him, although his exertions in the marsh did him no harm since he died aged ninety in 1976. There is a group painting of Sir John and his fellow members of the Tarporley Hunt Club in their livery, a copy of which I spotted hanging in a tailor's shop in Savile Row. Otherwise, his presence on earth was attended by no event of consequence apart from the birth of his son and heir who became a Royal Navy Captain.

David Tang

One day in May 1980 I received a letter, elegantly handwritten, from a David Tang, then unknown to me. The writer congratulated us on the award of two offshore oil licences in the South China Sea and the Yellow Sea; asserted that we should now require an English-speaking Chinese on our staff; and advised that *he* should be that Chinese. I filed it in the wastepaper basket until shortly afterwards our mutual friend, Annunziata Asquith, at that time a successful art dealer specialising in Oriental art, told me firmly that I was an idiot not to meet David as 'he is quite special and different.' Accordingly, I did, and there began for him a period of employment but, for both of us, a long-standing friendship.

In the course of our negotiations with the Chinese National Offshore Oil Corporation (CNOOC) they despatched a delegation from Beijing to Europe in 1981. This was headed by the director, You De Hua, and included lawyers, geologists and engineers. The ruthless application of Chairman Mao's 'Cultural' Revolution edicts had led to the virtual elimination of a generation of the intelligentsia, with the result that the composition of this delegation were either in their twenties or very much older. Of the latter, there was a really ancient gentleman – Mr Wu – who had a pre-1914 hearing aid consisting of a large wooden box and a pair of headphones which he clamped to his head during the meetings but who, nonetheless, made no contribution to the discussions. At a dinner I gave on the first evening (they always ate at 6pm and preferred to be in bed by 8pm) I asked You De Hua what role Mr Wu played in CNOOC.

'Oh, Mr Wu is very important, he is an expert in capitalism!' he asserted.

I asked him how he had become so expert.

'Mr Wu lived in America in 1926,' he replied firmly.

***

David Tang, after education at the Perse School in Cambridge and articles at a London firm of solicitors, left for Beijing where he taught students English at Beijing University. He realised that the Cultural Revolution was in its death throes and he wanted to be involved with his homeland when at last it started dealing with capitalism again.

David, who died recently aged only sixty-three, was the grandson of the founder of KMB (the famous Kowloon Motor Bus Company) – Sir S.Y. Tang. Legend has it that David's father committed the serious solecism of having an affair with Sir S.Y.'s mistress. In any event, he fled to England where he became effectively a professional gambler. David had the melancholy experience of finding his father dead in his bed at his flat in Chelsea Harbour.

David spent a short time at our London office, helping with those expert Chinese capitalists, but was clearly anxious to get to Hong Kong as soon as possible. It quickly became evident that David was a man in a hurry. I always sensed that he knew his life was to be a short one which was, to me, the explanation for his almost manic energy. That energy was complemented by his generosity, his intelligence and his irrepressible humour.

We had many adventures together in Beijing which, in the early 1980s, was a spartan city to say the least. We were never quite sure whether his presence – clad in a pin-striped Savile Row suit and chain-smoking Havana cigars – was a great help with the Chairman Mao-suited communist apparatchiks, but he certainly rendered it all the greatest fun. Before he left London for Hong Kong, my most junior employee had introduced me to philosophers such as Bryan Magee, Professor Freddie Ayer and Isaiah Berlin; to Roald Dahl, not to mention the Lord Chancellor and numerous legendary beauties. By the time he returned to Hong Kong, there to open an office, we had funded our exploration activities thanks to the support of: Inchcape; Wheelock Marden; Sir Y. K. Pao; Michael Sandberg at the (then) Hong Kong & Shanghai Bank and Li Ka-Shing, whose two remaining senior non-Chinese executives – George Magnus and Simon Murray – became lifelong friends of mine, with Simon being a particularly close friend and co-adventurer of David's.

Having opened our Hong Kong office in the Jardine building, we decided that we should take further advantage of China's race for development by looking at non-oil opportunities. This evolved into Cluff Investment and Trading. We were joined by the formidable Tessa Keswick and, incredibly, by Premier Foods of South Africa in the form of Albert Nelissen and Arne Glucksman – both of whom, it appeared, were actually employed by the Israeli secret service.

We signed exclusive (we thought) trade deals with Wenzhou and Ning Po and had a merry time without really getting anywhere. Tessa's enthusiasm for investment and trading was somewhat muted by waking up in her Wenzhou hotel room to discern a rat the size of a Cadillac perched on the end of her bed!

At about this time, David's grandfather died leaving David a legacy which provided for him to go it alone. So the Cluff Oil office became Cluff and Tang, then Tang and Cluff and then Tang! But we remained the closest friends whilst he began his meteoric ascent to celebrity.

David was an entrepreneur, an impresario and a kind of genius at mixing commerce and culture. His first essays into business were Shanghai Tang and the China Club, both located in Hong Kong. In both cases, David cleverly looked to the old China, of which he was so proud, for inspiration. Although making full use of it, David was repelled by the contemporary Chinese obsession with new technology, and so Shanghai Tang celebrated traditional Chinese costume; whilst the China Club – providing outstanding Chinese cuisine complemented by the finest European wine – was really a reversal of the clock to 1930s Shanghai: traditional Chinese furniture, silverware and white table cloths, with the staff all wearing white tunics. Traditional Chinese paintings were not an option, so David exhibited his genius again by displaying modern and contemporary Chinese art – in particular, the exhilarating political and military art of the Cultural Revolution. In this regard, he sought the advice of Johnson Chang, an art academic turned dealer. This formula he replicated with similar clubs in Beijing and Singapore.

During this highly productive period, David's first marriage failed, probably due to the constant pressure and rate at which he lived. Susannah was a Chinese-Australian actress of great charm and beauty who bore him a son, Edward, and a daughter, Victoria. She developed cancer and, seriously ill, her Indian surgeon not only married his patient but also cured her. David then married Lucy Wastnage – an English beauty with whom he shared many adventures and who was by his side until the end.

In 1982, I became aware of a house in the Sei Kung area of the new territories that an English stockbroker with the firm of James Capel wished to sell. By this time, the legendary factotum – Alex – had joined David's staff. Alex and David became a team celebrated throughout Hong Kong. Alex, six feet tall and tough, became the perfect foil for David's fulminations as Alex drove him round the then colony in an open Rolls-Royce. One Saturday morning, Alex drove David and me to inspect the Sei Kung house. 'If you don't buy it, I will!' I goaded David, for it was indeed in a delightful position, if deficient in architectural charm. David immediately realised its potential, bought it and reoriented the rooms to face the peaceful island-studded waters. It was to become an important extension to David – all about books, music, cooking and Labradors, one cheekily named 'Algy', which lived in the office during the period he worked for Cluff Oil ('Come here Algy, you lazy bastard!' David frequently intoned whilst standing next to me). Many were the happy days I spent at Sei Kung, including the nights before my marriage in St Stephen's Chapel. Sei Kung became famous for David's lunch parties on the terrace and I have vivid memories of David and his closer friends: Simon Murray, David Davies and Charles Letts, along with any visitor to Hong Kong of consequence – the criterion being style rather than importance.

In September 1993, I got married in Hong Kong. I was fifty-three and it was my first marriage. My wife is twenty years younger and was keen that we should have a traditional church wedding. The thought of walking up the aisle aged fifty-three in an English country church with my friends sniggering was not appealing, so I suggested that we got married in Hong Kong and asked David to be the best man and find a suitable church. I did not propose inviting anyone other than friends who lived there. David proposed St Stephen's Chapel in the fishing village of Stanley, where the chapel was the centrepiece of the local Protestant school. (The Stanley peninsula had been selected by the invading Japanese in 1942 to base the largest prisoner of war camp for mostly European prisoners. It had also been the grim site of the massacre of twenty British nurses and the cemetery contains the graves of many ill-nourished prisoners who died, as well as the graves of some heroic individuals who were murdered by their captors. The chapel had been constructed by the prisoners.)

The day before the wedding, David gave a lunch for the Governor – Chris Patten – and me, and that evening he threw a dinner at his famed China Club for about twenty friends including Henry and Simon Keswick, James Filmer-Wilson, the Liu Lit Man family, Evelyn Cromer, Simon Murray, Andrew Devonshire and Julian Reid (whose daughter Sarah, my god-daughter, was a bridesmaid). Henry Keswick 'gave' my wife away. We had a short rehearsal during which a smell of burning arose from the altar on which David had placed his cigar! It was exceptionally hot and as we entered the chapel typhoon storm signal no. 7 was being hoisted, which led me to ponder what sort of omen that was for our marriage... After the service, Alex drove us in the Rolls to No. 9 Shek O – the handsome bungalow owned by Jardine Matheson overlooking the South China Sea. To me there could be no more romantic setting for a honeymoon, abbreviated as it was, as I set off two days later (with my wife) on a business trip to Beijing and to the Chinese National Offshore Oil Company.

David's manifold talents evolved at this time and I would characterise the most important of them as: the pleasure of reading and collecting books; of music, both as pianist and enthusiast; of gambling, about which I am happily ignorant; of shooting; and of clubs.

David really loved his books and his offices and houses rejoiced in them. They were everywhere, except on the ceiling! Cyril Connolly produced a book in 1965 called *The Modern Movement* that listed one hundred key books from England, America and France from 1880–1960. David instructed Nicholas Dunne, the managing director of the Heywood Hill bookshop, to acquire all one hundred of

Connolly's collection. I cherish many volumes given to me by David – mostly works of reference and handsomely bound. David's presents ranged from Wodehouse to Waugh and the philosophers. David could hold his own in any abstract conversation. His personal brand of philosophical fatalism enabled him to remain cheerful until the end.

I am not sure precisely when David began shooting, but he rapidly became a first-class shot. With his custom-made Range Rover and his highly idiosyncratic wardrobe, David became a familiar figure at Britain's leading shooting estates. Many of these shoots he rented, and so many of his shooting friends enjoyed his generosity. His criterion was cheerful companionship as much as shooting prowess. Of the shoots I would judge Alnwick, Garrowby, the Lakes, Blenheim and Arundel as amongst his favourites. Of his guests, Henry Strutt, Sunny Marlborough and his son Jamie, Dave Ker, Roddie Fleming, Brian Williamson, Vivien Duffield, Julian Seymour and many others enjoyed his largesse.

David, of course, was nothing if not gregarious and clubs played a large part in his life. He belonged to many, but his undoubted favourite was White's, the oldest – and still arguably the best. On 22nd June 2017, he gave a lunch there for me to mark an award I had received. I think that must have been the last time he held court in his customary style, keeping all his guests on their toes.

Music, I have no doubt, governed David's life more than anything (other than his family). At one point in the 1980s he was due to play a Brahms concerto with the Hong Kong Philharmonic. Alas, en route to the concert hall, Alex drove the Rolls into a traffic light, rendering both the car and the musician temporarily disabled.

David maintained his remarkable and remorseless career as entrepreneur and impresario through the beginning of the 21st century and, indeed, added another dimension: that of agony uncle in the Saturday issue of the *Financial Times*. This, required reading for many, was characteristically unique in its combination of irascible exasperation and humour, whilst revealing the deep reservoir of his knowledge.

However, whilst he continued to add enduring new entrepreneurial conquests, in particular the restaurant China Tang in the Dorchester Hotel, to his portfolio, it was apparent that all was not well, manifested by his fluctuating physique and increasing immobility. The latter led to him being recommended to have a hip replacement operation in 2016. Preliminary blood tests revealed the grim news that he had cancer of the liver, necessitating an immediate liver replacement operation in China. From thereon, he waged a constant battle for life. Notwithstanding his suffering, he retained his exemplary generosity and his relentless curiosity. Above all, humour remained his companion until the end. He gave so much to so many on so many levels that the word unique seems somehow inadequate.

Rupert Deen

About twenty years ago, Rupert was appointed the foreman, by his fellow jurors, at the trial of the notorious Charlie Richardson – leader of a criminal gang of torturers and bank robbers. Apart from being Rupert's sole pro bono contribution to society, the jury-room discussions involved, to the other jurors' amazement, a defence of the accused from Rupert himself. When the foreman was challenged as to how it were possible for him to speak up for such a palpable criminal as Richardson, Rupert remarked 'Oh, I thought he was rather a sportsman!'

This statement of course exemplified Rupert's anarchic personality and his endearing inability to see wrong in anyone he liked, and was amongst the reasons he had such a huge reservoir of friends.

Rupert was born in 1938 and his family and background is of some interest. Rupert's grandfather, Emile, together with his seven great uncles, set the scene for the eventual merger of the Royal Dutch Company and the Shell Oil company by brokering the pooling of gasoline supplies, storage facilities and marketing. Of Dutch origin – although Emile lived in Paris – they were adroit oil traders and a force to be reckoned with in the early days of oil production in what was then, pre-First World War, the Dutch East Indies. Alas, in 1925 a feud erupted between Royal Dutch Shell – the brainchild of Marcus Samuel, 1st Viscount Bearsted – and the Deen family who were sued for the colossal sum (in 1925) of £50 million. The history of Shell by Henriquez is silent on this matter, but Rupert's uncle – Maurice – although only twenty-five at the time, contrived to reduce the damages to zero. Ironically, I recall that Rupert, never one to bear a grudge, regularly rented the Bearsted villa during various Monaco grand prix – the most important date in Rupert's calendar.

To understand Rupert, it is necessary to place him in this context of wealth and privilege which obtained during his youth. It is also necessary to refer to his parents – Frank and Joan. I first met Rupert in 1959 at their then family home – Little Heath House – near Berkhamsted. It exuded an oriental atmosphere with teak furniture, gongs and carved elephants all over the place. His mother Joan bore a strong resemblance to Mrs Wilberforce, the dear old lady in the film *The Ladykillers*. She was rumoured to have cherished the notion that Rupert might one day become a ballet dancer! Frank was the image of Rupert: handsome, charming and good-natured. Also like his son in that he was devoid of a scintilla of ambition and sailed serenely through life, treating work with the same apprehension we might apply to ill health. In this regard, I should say that Frank was quite unlike his brother Maurice – a dynamic figure who founded the Blue Star garages empire. What they had in common were two huge houses in Beaulieu-sur-Mer, Frank's oddly named the 'Villa Le Petit'.

The first occasion I stayed there, I, for some reason, was to arrive the day before Rupert and his parents – 'Just ring the bell on the gate and André the gardener will welcome you and show you to your room' Rupert assured me. I duly carried out these instructions, rang the bell, André appeared and said, 'If you don't go away I will fetch my gun!' I went away, returned the next day and spent a week that I can recall vividly now, fifty years on. The party included Rupert and John Deen, Brian Alexander, Madeleine Rampling and Patrick Lichfield. Mrs Deen would bustle about, dressed always in black, ensuring we all had whatever we needed. Frank, meanwhile, started the day off with a bang, reading what was then called the *Continental Daily Mail*, from cover to cover, then retiring to his study for a rest before lunch. This was an attractive octagonal room in the midst of which was an enormous desk. Frank sat at the desk with an uncharacteristic frown on his handsome face. After five days, I said to him: 'What are you doing, Frank? Working on some scheme or other?' He replied, 'No, I am trying to remember the combination of the safe.' In the safe, it appeared, was an important letter that had to be retrieved. After seven days the sun burst through, Frank's frown evaporated. He had remembered the combination: 1234!

There were many other happy holidays in that wonderful house with excursions to David Niven's villa and every five-star restaurant on the Riviera. One weekend, a member of our aristocracy brought no less than Christine Keeler to stay, causing Mrs Deen much welcome consternation. Alas the house finally had to go and is now a block of flats, but I am sure the benign ghosts of Frank, Joan and Rupert will always roam there.

Rupert was educated at Harrow where, if nothing else, he became a more than competent golfer and where he made enduring friendships with, in particular, Brian Alexander, Patrick Lichfield and John Pryor – the last a solicitor and an incongruous figure in Rupert's life, having a nine-to-five job – unique amongst Rupert's friends. Dr James, the headmaster of Harrow, some years later recalled Rupert as the laziest boy he had ever taught, although very far from stupid, he added.

After Harrow there occurred a long gap before the next event – membership of the British Olympic lugeing team in 1972. This sport was entirely suited to Rupert's requirements since it is the only sport which is conducted with the participant lying flat on his back.

I have a book, published in 1983, entitled *Who's Really Who*, in which Rupert features along with four hundred others. The author of this scholarly work explains in the introduction that he has selected 'achievers' who shine in whatever their field. It was with some interest accordingly that I read Rupert's 'field' was defined as that of a 'character', which is surely true. The article is accompanied by a photograph of our hero, with his Clark Gable moustache, looking very dashing. The author, having pointed out admiringly that Rupert spent only twenty-six days a year at the offices of Wright Deen, continues to select an example of the Deen philosophy: "'All I know," Rupert avers, "is that pheasants are reared to be shot, Labradors to retrieve them and Welshmen to go down coal mines.'"

Notwithstanding the boulevardier image Rupert assiduously cultivated, I think it is important to stress that, in fact, firstly he was an extraordinarily competent and modest sportsman, having represented his country not only at lugeing, but also at water-skiing and golf (he was a scratch player). And secondly, he *chose* not to work, but had he done so I am certain that his natural shrewdness would have rendered him successful.

Although Rupert did nothing to secure approbation in a conventional sense, he brought sunshine and gaiety into many lives and his friends have cause to thank him for adding so much to the rich tapestry of life.

The Remembrance Trust

I AM NOW of an age which becomes inevitably melancholy by reason of the death of contemporaries. I am of a retiring disposition, although clubbable, and have not found it easy to forge new friendships outside of my business life. This problem, however, has been greatly mitigated by my good fortune in enjoying a late marriage which has borne me three boys whom I now count as the replacement for those friends I have lost.

Barring one resourceful lady (ninety-six) all my parents' generation are now deceased. Many of my father's contemporaries, of course, died in the First World War before they were even adults – my uncle was killed aged seventeen at Gallipoli, for example. The Second World War had justifiable cause, but recent disastrous excursions – Vietnam, Iraq, Afghanistan and Libya – demonstrate the inability of politicians to understand issues or recognise their limitations. Sir Robert Walpole was able to report to Queen Anne in 1714: '50,000 men killed in Europe this year, your Majesty, and not one of them an Englishman.' Would that Mr Blair and Mr Cameron reported similarly.

It is the soldiers who die, never the politicians. All around the world graves and their memorials attest to their sacrifice. It is not generally understood that the brief of the incomparable Commonwealth War Graves Commission applies only to those killed from 1914 onwards. No graves or memorials prior to that are anyone's responsibility, unless regiments or families elect to assume it, and in reality few are able to do so. Having served for eleven years as the Chairman of the UK War Memorials Trust until 2014, I now propose to establish a new charity dedicated to the restoration and preservation of those older graves and memorials around the world. The proceeds from this book will be applied in support of this new charity.

Acknowledgements

I THANK THE sons of Sir John Grandy, Bill and John, for the loan of the photograph of their father 'in the cockpit'; Ursula Hollis for the loan of the book of remembrance of her uncle Charles Parish DFC, compiled by his father; Brigadier Andrew Parker-Bowles for the loan of photographs in his collection, which rivals that of Geoffrey Keating for its quality and for its skilful record of the upper levels of British class life in the latter part of the twentieth- and the early twenty-first centuries; Briggie Freeman, for the photograph of her late husband, Nicholas, by Patrick Lichfield; and to Gavin Stamp for the photograph of *The Spectator*'s staff excursion to Glasgow. I am grateful to John Beveridge QC for his generous legal advice on this and many other occasions.

Index

Aegean Adventures 7
Alexander, Brian 132, 134
Alexander, William 17
All to the Good 96
Allcock, Agnes 22
Allsopp, Charlie, 6th Baron Hindlip 41
Ancona, Matthew d' 99-100
Annabel's nightclub 87
Anson, Patrick, 5th Earl of Lichfield 56, 133, 134
Arcangues, Guy, Marquis d' 109-10
As I Was Going to St Ives 26
Asquith, Lady Annunziata 118

Associated Newspapers 53
Attlee, Clement, 1st Earl Attlee, 16
Ayer, Professor Freddie 121

Baring, Evelyn, 4th Earl of Cromer 125
Baring, Mona 60
Barlows 105
Barnato family 71
Bearsted, Lord *see* Samuel, Marcus
Beatty, Sir Alfred Chester 71-2
Beatty, Chet 71
Beaufort, David, *see* Somerset, David
Beckett, Angus 49-53,

63
Beer, Claude 89-90
Beit family 71
Bellville, Rupert 91
Benn, Tony 61, 62
Berlin, Sir Isaiah 121
Berry, Alexander 103
Berry, Colonel Julian 44
Berry, Michael, Lord Hartwell 104
Berry, Nicholas 102-109
Berry, William 103
Berry, William, 1st Viscount Camrose 103
Bevan, Rt. Hon. Aneurin 30-31
Beveridge, John 19-20, 21-22
Beveridge, Professor W. I. B. 19-20
Bigoray, Flight Sergeant 28-9
Bingham, Richard, 7th Earl of Lucan 90
Birch, Nigel, Baron Rhyl 68
Birks, Dr Jack 55
Birley, Lady Annabel 87

Birley, Mark 80-81, 87
Boodle's Club 45, 68
Booker, Christopher 98
Boyle, Captain Michael 'Docker' 45-7
BP 52, 55, 61, 86-7
Brand, Mickie 10-14
British Airways 41, 82, 84
British American Tobacco 76
British National Oil Corporation 62
Britten, Colonel Pat 31
Broad, Lieutenant Richard 86
Brook Club 83-4
Brooke, Lord David 12, 13-14
Brooks's Club 79, 89, 91
Butler, Basil 55

Cable and Wireless 90
Cambridge University 19-20, 50
Castro, Fidel 79
Cathcart, Alan, 6th Earl Cathcart 75
Cavalry Club 112

Cavendish, Andrew, 11th Duke of Devonshire 125
Cavendish, Henry 83
CCP North Sea Associates 56, 58-62
Cecil, Charles 112
Centre for Policy Studies 113-14
Cetawayo, King 70
Chancellor, Alexander 98
Chang, Johnson 123
Charterhall 58-9
Chase Ritts, Leonard (III) 58
Chataway, Christopher 66
Chataway, Miss 66-7
Chater Collection 17-19
Chater, Sir Paul 16-17, 18
Chiang Kai-Shek 15-16
Chichester-Clark, Major James, Baron Moyola 43-4
China Club 122-3
Chinese National Offshore Oil Corporation 118-19
Chinnery, George 17
Churchill, Rt. Hon. Sir Winston 2, 3, 15, 25
Clarke, Rt. Hon. Kenneth 113
Clerk, Sir George 13
Clermont Club 11, 87
Cluff, Blondel 124
Cluff Investment and Trading 121-22
Cluff Oil 62, 122
Cold War 35, 37
Coldstream Guards 10, 59
Collins, Neil 107
Commonwealth War Graves Commission 137
Connolly, Cyril 126
Constant Heart, A 92
Contades, Arnaud 103
Contades, Comte Arnold de 103
Cook, Rt. Hon. Robin 21
Cooper, Duff, 1st Viscount Norwich 92-3
Cooper, Kevin 59

Cooper, Peter A. V. 59-60
Cornwall-Jones, Paul 96, 97
Craven-Walker, Tony 62
Cromer, Evelyn *see* Baring, Evelyn 125
Cuba 78-80, 104
Cyprus 30-32

Dahl, Roald 121
Davidson, Duncan 75
Davies, Sir David 124
de Valera, Éamon 71-2
Deen, Emile 131
Deen, Frank 131-3
Deen, Joan 131-3
Deen, John 132
Deen, Maurice 131, 132
Deen, Rupert 35, 130-35
Deepdale Golf Club 75
Delves-Broughton, Rosie, Lady Lovat 111
Derby, John *see* Stanley, Edward John
Devonshire, Andrew *see* Cavendish, Andrew
Dickson, David 34

Dixon, Sir John 116-17
Docker, Sir Bernard 45
Docker, Lady Norah 45
Dohm, Chris 54, 58
Double Traverse of Vatnajokull, The 50
Douglas-Hamilton, George, 10th Earl of Selkirk 33
Duffield, Dame Vivien 127
Dunne, Nicholas 126

Editions Alecto 96-7
Edsor, Simon 98
El Oro 6
Elliott, Elsie 21
Ellis, Fred 66
Exploration Company 6
Eykyn, Jamie 32

Fallon, Ivan 66, 106
Fane, David, 15th Earl of Westmorland 33-4
Fildes, Christopher 84, 105, 107
Fildes, Richard 105, 107
Filmer-Wilson, James 125

Financial Times 128
Firmston-Williams, Lady Heather 41-2
First World War 16, 83, 100-101, 117, 136
Fischer, Harry 11
Fleet, Kenneth 66
Fleming, Roddie 127
Foot, Rt. Hon. Sir Dingle 30
Foot, Hugh, Baron Caradon 30, 31-2
Foot, Rt. Hon. Michael 30
Fortune, General Victor 85-6
Fox-Strangways, Lt Charles Stephen 30-31
Fox-Strangways, John 30-31
Fraser, Robert 96
Fraser, W. Lionel 96
Freeman, Jemma 78
Freeman, Councillor Nicholas 81
Freeman, Nicholas 78-81
Freeman, Robert 78

Gage, Nicky, 8th Viscount Gage 11

Gater, Sir George 16
Gestetner, Jonathan 12
Getty, J. Paul 51
Gibraltar 8, 33, 36
Gloag, Matthew 99
Glucksman, Arne 121
Goldsmith, Annabel *see* Birley, Lady Annabel
Goldsmith, Jimmy 76
Gormley, Joe 63-4
Gould, Diana, Baroness Menuhin 19
Grandy, Sir John, Marshal of the Royal Air Force 33, 35-7
Greene, Graham 98-9
Grenadier Guards 24, 31, 32
Grierson, Jacob 42
Grierson, Sir Ronald 38-42
Griffiths, Attorney General John 21
Grundon, John 56
Guards Parachute Company 33
Gulbenkian collection 72
Gunn, Herbert James 2

Hambros Bank 80
Hamilton, Fred 53
Hamilton (oil company) 52-3, 54
Hamilton, Richard 96, 97
Hampshire Police Authority 45
Hanson, Lord James 42, 83
Harcourt, Admiral Sir Cecil 15-19
Harmsworth, Esmond, 2nd Viscount Rothermere 53-5
Hearne, Graham 62
Heath, Rt. Hon. Sir Edward 64, 65
Helbert Wagg 96
Henderson, Pam 60
Hilton, Anthony 66
Hockney, David 97
Hollis, Ursula 8-9
Honeyman Brown, Christopher 107
Hong Kong 15-22, 120-25, 128
Hopkins, Harry 3
Household Cavalry 30-32

Hoylake Group 76
Hunters and Frankau 80, 81

Inchcape 121
Irby, Paul 91-2
Irish Guards 45, 59

Jackson, Derek 26-7
Jagger, Sir Mick 96
James, Dr Robert 134
Jardine Matheson 126
Jerdein, Charles 96-7
Joel family 71
Johnson, Rt. Hon. Boris 99
Johnson, Dr Samuel 82
Johnston, Rt. Hon. Thomas 2-3
Jones, Allen 97
Jones, Professor R. V. 23-9
Jordan, Harold 27-9
Joseph, Sir Keith 113
Joseph, Leopold 11, 12

Keating, Major Geoffrey 85-7
Keating, Rima 86, 87

Keating, Suzi 87
Keeler, Christine 133
Kennedy, Joe 2-3
Kennedy, Ludovic 96
Ker, Dave 127
Keswick, Sir Henry 56, 74, 113, 125
Keswick, Simon 125
Keswick, Lady Tessa xvii, 56, 74, 111, 112-14, 121-2
Keyt, George 93
King, John, Baron King of Wartnaby xvii, 82-4
King, Lorna 83
Knox, James 98-100
Kobza, Eugene von Nagy 17-18
Kowloon Motor Bus Company 120
Kraan, Max 69

Lambton, Tony, 6th Earl of Durham 56, 60, 87
Lavery, Sir John 98
Letts, Charles 124
Lewis, David 80
Li Ka-Shing 121
Lichfield, Patrick *see* Anson, Patrick
Life Guards 43-4
Lindemann, Professor Frederick, Lord Cherwell 25-6
Lindsay, Patrick 34
Linning, Matt 55-6
Liu Lit Man family 125
Lockhart, Sir Robert Bruce 4
Lonrho 65
Lovat, Simon, 15th Baron Lovat 111-12
Lucan, Lord *see* Bingham, Richard
Lumley, Brigadier 92

M. B. P. Russell & Co. 94
McGovern, Father 21
MacLennan, Inspector John 20-22
Magee, Bryan 121
Magnus, George 121
Magnus-Allcroft, Sir Philip 33
Mail, Daily 66, 106, 133
Manchester Ship Canal 104-105

Manningham-Buller, Sir Reginald, 1st Viscount Dilhorne 67-8
Mansfield, Lord *see* Murray, William
Mao, Chairman 16, 119, 121
Marchessini, Alexander 57-8
Marchessini, Demetri 56-8, 111
Marchessini, Tati 57, 58
Margaret, Princess 12
Marie Claire 108-109, 110
Marlborough Fine Art 11, 12
Marlborough, Sunny, 11th Duke of Marlborough 54, 56, 74, 127
Marlowe, Suki 100
Martyn, Philip 89-90
Maxwell, Robert 90
Meehan, Mungo 84
Melchett, Lady Sonia 87
Memorial to the Missing on the Somme 100
Menuhin, Baron Yehudi 19

Mintel 104, 105-106
Modern Movement, The 126
Monkton, Isabel, Lady King of Wartnaby 83, 84
Montgomery, Field Marshal Bernard, 1st Viscount Montgomery of Alamein 86
Montmort, Donatienne de 108
Moore, Charles 99
Morton, Alastair 62
Muir, Robin 12
Munnings, Sir Alfred 44
Murchison, Mary, Viscountess Rothermere 53, 55
Murray, Simon 121, 124, 125
Murray, William, 8th Earl of Mansfield 75
Myers & Co. 59-60

Nelissen, Albert 121
Nelke, Maud 92
Nelson, Fraser 100
Niven, David 133
North Sea oil 1, 24, 40,

49-56, 58-64
Nuttall, Sir Nicholas, 3rd Baronet 32

Oil and Gas Authority 49, 62, 63
Oldfield, Sir Maurice 87
Onedin Line, The 23
O'Neill, Hugh, 3rd Baron Rathcavan 87
Oppenheimer family 70-71
Orange, James 17
Oxford University 6, 24, 70, 71, 97

Pacific Cigar Company 79
Packer, Kerry 76
Paget, Dorothy 96
Pakenham, Paddy 107
Pao, Sir Y. K. 121
Paolozzi, Sir Eduardo 97
Paravicini, Suki *see* Marlowe, Suki
Parish, Charles 5-6, 7-8
Parish, Clement Woodbine 6
Parish, Godfrey 5, 8-9

Parish, Major Michael Woodbine 5, 6
Parish, Robin 6-7
Parker, Hubert, Lord Justice, Baron Parker of Waddington 66, 67
Patrick, Andrew 98
Patten, Rt. Hon. Chris, Baron Patten of Barnes 125
Paulton, Pilot Officer 28-9
Peel Holdings 105
Pender, Lord Joss 90
Pennell, M. M. 55
Peto, Nicholas 58
Phillips, Nicholas 56
Phillips, Admiral Sir Tom 92-3
Private Eye 87
Prouvost, Jacques 102
Prouvost, Jean 102-103
Prouvost, Marie-Laure 108
Prouvost-Berry, Evelyne 102-103, 108-110
Pryor, John 134
Pumphrey, John 66-7

Queen's Guard 46

Raborn, Smiley 58
Rampling, Madeleine 132-3
Ranger Oil 52, 61
Rathcavan, Hugh *see* O'Neill, Hugh
Rawlings, Louis 114
Rawlings, Baroness Patricia 111, 114-15
Reay, Aeneas 113
Reay, Lord Hugh 56, 113
Reay, Laura 113
Reay, Ned 113
Reay, Lady *see* Keswick, Tessa
Reflections on Intelligence 25
Reid, Julian 125
Reid, Sarah 125
Remembrance Trust, The 101, 137
Rhodes, Cecil 69-71
Richardson, Charlie 130
Roberts, Lucinda 58
Robinson family 71
Roosevelt, President Franklin D. 2-3, 15, 16
Rothermere, Esmond, *see* Harmsworth, Esmond
Rowland, 'Tiny' 20, 65
Rowntree, Captain James 43-4
Royal Air Force 7-8, 27, 33, 35-6
Royal Dutch Company 131
Royal St George's Golf Club 60
Royal Yacht Squadron 33, 36-7, 45, 46, 75
Russell, Captain Ed 54
Russell, Emily 92
Russell, Gilbert 92
Russell, Martin 91-4
Russell, Serena 54
Ruttenberg, Derald 73-77
Ruttenberg, Janet 74-5

St James's Club 89-90, 95, 96
Salmond, Rt. Hon. Alex 1-2, 4
Samuel, Marcus, 1st Viscount Bearsted 131

Samuel, Marcus, 3rd Viscount Bearsted 41
Sandberg, Lord Michael 121
Second World War xvii, 2-3, 5-8, 15-16, 25-29, 35, 37-9, 59, 85-6, 90, 92-3, 109-110, 112, 125, 136
Selkirk, Geordie *see* Douglas-Hamilton, George
Sergeant, Patrick 66
Seymour, Sir Julian 127
Shanghai Tang 122
Sheehy, Sir Patrick 76, 79, 84
Shell Oil 42, 51, 52, 61, 90, 131
Shikar Club 112
Skelton, Barbara 26
Slessor, Air Marshal Sir John 31
Smallpeice, Sir Basil 65
Smith, F. E., 1st Earl of Birkenhead 6, 13, 103
Smith, Laura 12-13
Somerset, David, 11th Duke of Beaufort 11

South Africa 62, 70, 121
Spectator, The xv, 60-61, 84, 87, 98-100
Spencer-Churchill, Charles, 9th Duke of Marlborough 54, 56, 74, 127
Spencer-Churchill, James, 12th Duke of Marlborough 54, 127
Stamp, Professor Gavin 100-101
Stanley, Edward John, 18th Earl of Derby 74
Stapleton, David 34
Stoop, Adrian 90
Stoop, Michael 90
Stourton, Michael 31-32
Strutt, Henry, 5th Baron Belper 127
Studholme, Joe 96, 97
Sturgeon, Rt. Hon. Nicola 1

Tang, Sir David xvii, 79, 118, 119-29
Tang, Edward 123
Tang, Sir S.Y. 120
Tang, Susannah 123
Tang, Victoria 123

Tarporley Hunt Club 116, 117
Tebbit, Norman 84
Telegraph, Daily 103, 104
Tennant, Andrew 73
Thatcher, Rt. Hon. Baroness Margaret 62, 82
Thomas, George, 1st Viscount Tonypandy 99
Thyssen collection 72
Tillotson, Alan 34-5
Tillotson, John 34-5
Tillotson, Marcus 34-5
Transworld Petroleum 54, 56, 58
Truant Disposition, A 41
Truman, President Harry 16
Tucker, Geoffrey 64

Vasarely, Victor 97
Villiers, Nicholas 56, 79
Vink, Peter de 1
Vyner, Henry 11, 12

Wallace, Billy 12

Wallace, Chisholm 112
Wallace, Hamish 112
Walpole, Sir Robert 137
War Memorials Trust xv, 100, 137
Ward, Peter 12
Wastnage, Lucy 123
Webster, Sir David 35
Weeks, John 105-106
Weinstock, Arnold 40-41
Weir, Willie, 1st Viscount Weir 76
Wernher family 71
Westmorland, David *see* Fane, David
Wheelock Marden 121
Whicker, Alan 87
Whistler, Rex 92
Whitbread, H. 'Loopy' 94-5
White, Gordon, Baron White of Hull 83
White's Club 12, 31, 44. 68, 83, 91, 127-8
Who's Really Who 134
Wigram, Anthony 56
Williamson, Sir Brian 127

Wilson, A. N. 100, 101
Wilson, Harold 67
Wilton, John, Earl of Wilton 12
Wolfson, David 114
Wu, Mr 119
Wyldbore-Smith, Major-General Sir Brian 33

Yang, T. L. 21
Yardley, Sergeant Tom 46
You De Hua 119
Young, Sir Mark 17-8

Zimbabwe 6, 69, 70

> Algy Cluff
>
> # Get On With It
> ### A Memoir
>
> FOREWORD BY
> A. N. Wilson

From the Foreword by A. N. Wilson

> There's nothing worth the wear of winning,
> But laughter and the love of friends

'Algy's life bears this out. This book is the opposite of a misery memoir. It rejoices in his kind parents, his good friends and his happy marriage with three splendid sons. His boldness in the field of business and his merriment as a companion have their reward.'